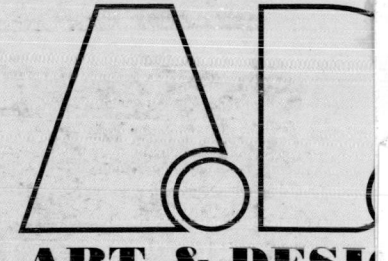

ART & DESIGN

ACADEMY GROUP LTD
42 LEINSTER GARDENS, LONDON
TEL: 0171-402 2141 FAX: 0171-7

HOUSE EDITOR: Nicola Hodges F
TEAM: Ramona Khambatta, Kather
MacInnes SENIOR DESIGNER: And
Bettella DESIGN CO-ORDINATOR: I
Bettella DESIGN TEAM: Jacqueline
Grosvenor, Gregory Mills

SUBSCRIPTION OFFICES:
UK: ACADEMY GROUP LTD
42 LEINSTER GARDENS
LONDON W2 3AN
TEL: 0171 402 2141 FAX: 0171-723

USA AND CANADA: VCH PUBLISHE
333 SEVENTH AVENUE, FIFTH FLOO
NEW YORK, NY 10001, USA
TEL: (212) 629 6200 FAX: (212) 629 8140

ALL OTHER COUNTRIES:
VCH VERLAGSGESELLSCHAFT MBH
BOSCHSTRASSE 12, POSTFACH 101161
69451 WEINHEIM
FEDERAL REPUBLIC OF GERMANY
TEL: 06201 606 148 FAX: 06201 606 184

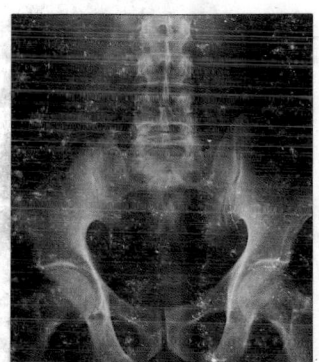

Nat Goodden, Detail of Bound-
ary Layer, 1993, x-ray

... um,

... 9

... hael ... Situ •
*Andrew **Benjamin*** Matter and Meaning: On In-
stallations • *Corinne **Diserens*** Gordon Matta-
Clark • *James **Turrell*** • *Jean-François **Lyotard***
Reserves of Spatial Events ***Arakawa** and*
*Madeline **Gins*** Landing Sites/The End of
Spacetime • *Richard **Artschwager*** • *Donald **Judd***
• *Cady **Noland*** • *Anya **Gallaccio*** • *Andrew **Sabin*** •
*Wolfgang **Laib*** • *Judith **Barry*** • *Joseph **Kosuth***

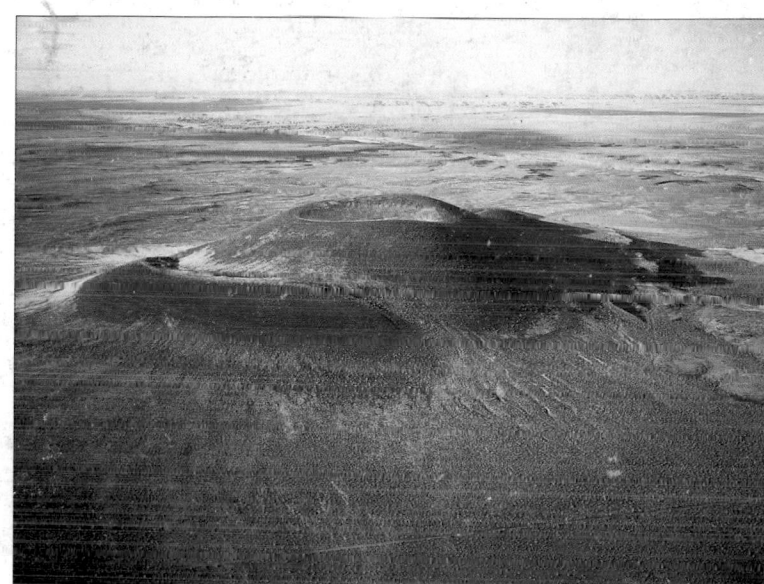

*James Turrell, Aerial View of the
Roden Crater Project, 1991*

NAT **GOODDEN**

MONA **HATOUM**

VONG **PHAOPHANIT**

GLADSTONE **THOMPSON**

Four Rooms

SERPENTINE GALLERY

FOREWORD

*Four Rooms** is an exhibition of installation work. Four artists have been commissioned to create installations in each of the Serpentine Gallery's four rooms. The works respond in very different ways to the architecture of the building, yet central to them all is the direct physical involvement of the spectator. The exhibition is, therefore, an opportunity to present four artists whose work, by transforming the space, challenges the visitor's perception of the Gallery.

Nat Goodden has channelled all access to the square, domed North Gallery up a staircase towards a viewing platform, which encircles the gallery at a height of four metres. From this lofty perspective the viewer looks down onto an intersecting network of translucent veils made up from hundreds of sheets of hospital x-rays.

In contrast to this complex and spectacular installation, Gladstone Thompson has made a quiet, austere but equally challenging intervention in the South Gallery. By enveloping with sheets of plywood the central walls and ceiling of this difficult ambulatory (corridor) space, which includes six doorways, he anchors the room, giving it a defined centre.

Mona Hatoum has drained the long West Gallery of all natural light, turning it into a windowless, claustrophobic room, illuminated only by a slowly moving naked bulb. Casting light on rows of cage-like lockers the bulb creates dramatic shadows on the surrounding walls which heighten the sense of dislocation and imprisonment. *Light Sentence* was originally conceived for an exhibition of Hatoum's work at Chapter, in Cardiff, and has also been presented at Arnolfini, in Bristol.

Vong Phaophanit's installation in the East Gallery also uses light to create a distinctive environment. By placing long, thin strips of red neon directly onto the floor and covering them with rice, his installation evokes associations of ploughed fields. Phaophanit conjures up memories of his home in Laos which he has not seen since 1973.

Our particular thanks go to the artists for responding so imaginatively to the Serpentine's invitation. Without their commitment and hard work it would have been impossible to have achieved such dramatic changes to the Gallery. We are also grateful to SGB Scaffolding for generously sponsoring *Boundary Layer* by Nat Goodden, to The Rice Bureau for providing long grain, white rice for *Neon Rice Field* by Vong Phaophanit, and to Matt's Gallery and Laure Genillard Gallery for their help.

Academy Group Ltd has once again collaborated with us by printing our exhibition catalogue and incorporating it into *Art and Design* magazine. We are grateful to John Stoddart and Nicola Hodges for their continuing support. Our thanks also go to James Roberts for his thoughtful catalogue essay.

Julia Peyton-Jones
Director, Serpentine Gallery

Andrea Schlieker
Assistant Director, Serpentine Gallery

* *Four Rooms* at the Serpentine Gallery should be distinguished from a touring exhibition of the same name organised by the Arts Council of Great Britain in 1984, which opened at Liberty, London and toured to Wolverhampton, Southampton, Newport, Aberdeen and Sheffield.

A ROOM WITH A VIEW
JAMES ROBERTS

Kensington Gardens has an air of the mythical about it – a sort of Empire-made Mount Olympus of Victorian England. Wendy, John and Michael Darling played in it before being whisked off to Never-Never Land by Peter Pan, and Dr Watson strolled through it on his way home to Notting Hill after adventuring out with Sherlock Holmes. In visual terms too, the park is no less full of incident: the Albert Memorial rises up in byzantine-gothic glory, or at least it used to before being disguised as a skyscraper, a Henry Moore sculpture pokes through the trees beside the Serpentine lake to remind you to think of nature and there is a round pond that isn't round at all. Then there is the Serpentine Gallery itself: once a tea pavilion and now a home for less frivolous pursuits. Surrounded by green lawns, its rooms are filled with light that enters through the numerous skylights punctuating the ceiling like a colander. Two of the walls are entirely composed of French windows, so that the park is almost as much in the building as the building is in the park. Like so much else in Kensington Gardens, the Gallery is a curious mixture of the artificial and the natural, the cultivated and the studiously casual. Whilst walking through the gardens it all appears unplanned and a little bit confused: paths seemingly meander across it to no particularly well-defined end and the tree planting can seem somewhat random to say the least. But, at a certain moment, this garden of the arbitrary suddenly slips into place as you turn a corner or catch a new viewpoint of the surroundings. Everything falls into alignment and the trees snap into neat rows lining either side of walkways whose directions and intersections now make perfect sense.

In a rather oblique way, Vong Phaophanit's installation, *Neon Rice Field* echoes something of this transformation from chaos to order and there is a curious relationship between the formality of his installation and the hidden order of the park's arrangement. From outside, an expanse of rice spread out on the floor is visible through the windows, but on entering the space, the mounds and troughs reveal themselves to be an arrangement of parallel lines whose peaks are picked out in lines of warm orange neon stretching back across the room to the rear wall. The image that springs to mind is one of furrows of a ploughed field: as if the rice had transformed itself back into the earth from which it came. In an unexpected combination of the organic and the synthetic, the bars of neon light glimmer from under this field of rice. This light suggests a dormant energy lurking in the ground waiting to be released, like the seeds themselves which contain a spark of life that might one day be released through germination. It is hard not to think of rice as being the staple diet for at least half the world's population and this agricultural reverie bears relation with the past of Kensington Gardens, which has progressed from being arable land, to pasture for sheep and finally the park, designed for pleasure, that we see today.

As a material, the rice has an extraordinary quality of translucency, in that it absorbs and seems to concentrate the light before releasing it again: the brighter the outside light becomes, the purer and whiter the rice appears. It is affected by the ambient light in the Gallery as much as by the neon within it, and it is difficult to tell whether these strips of light are coming from inside the rice mound or are being projected onto the surface. At a certain moment during the day there is such a perfect balance between the two light sources that the warm glow appears to be floating on the surface of the work. Much of Phaophanit's work has involved light, either projected, absorbed or condensed, with a combination of man-made and natural materials. In *Fragments*, exhibited at 'The British Art Show' in 1990, snapshot images were projected onto the revolving blades of electric fans, evoking the flickering, insubstantial nature of memory: a well-remembered detail here, a colour there, but nothing solid on which to base these flashes of reminiscence. What is seen in *Fragments* is literally the light itself, as the support on which it is projected is never station-

OPPOSITE: Vong Phaophanit, Neon Rice Field, *1993, installation at the Serpentine Gallery, London, neon, rice, dimensions of gallery: 6.7 x 11.0m*

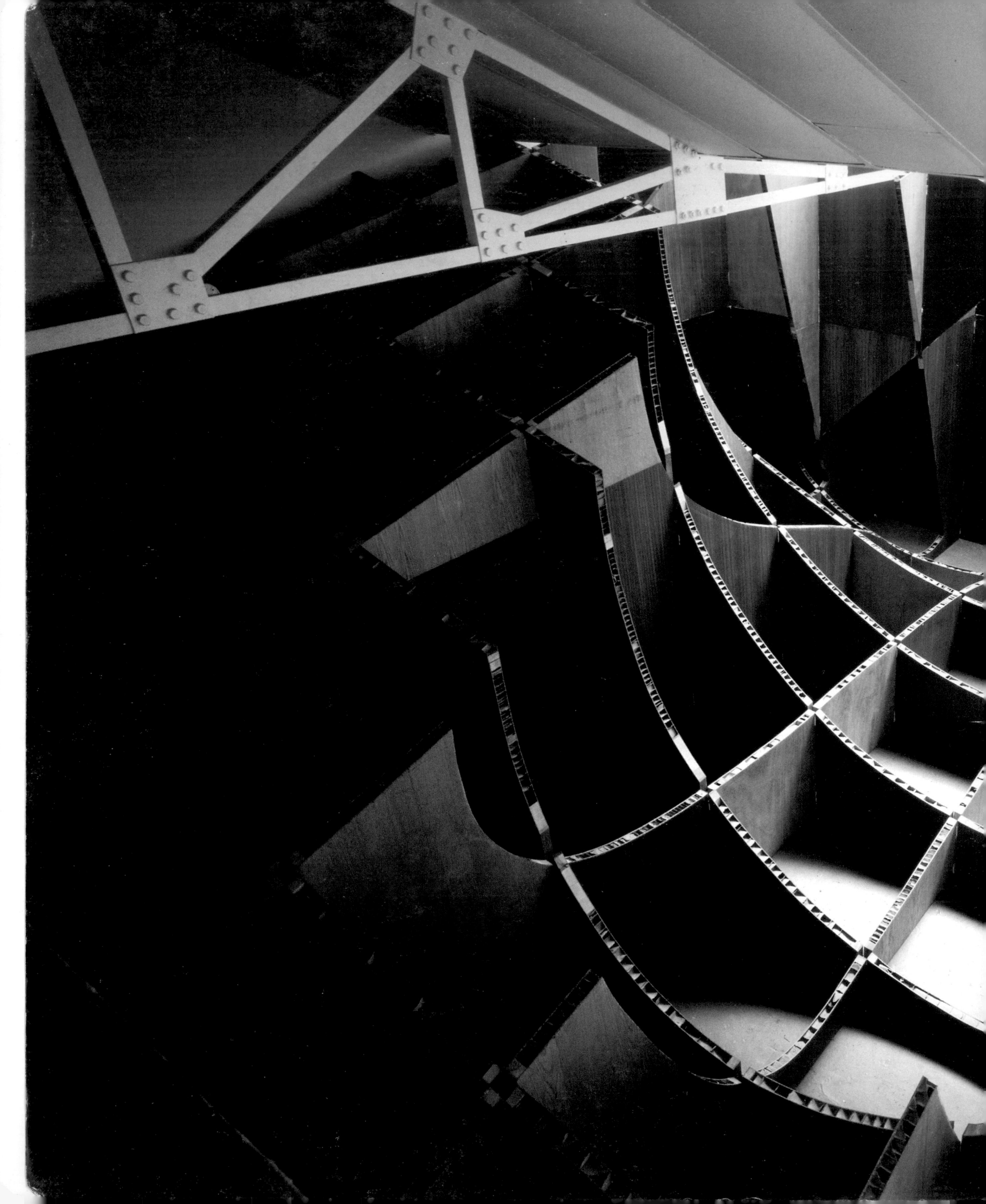

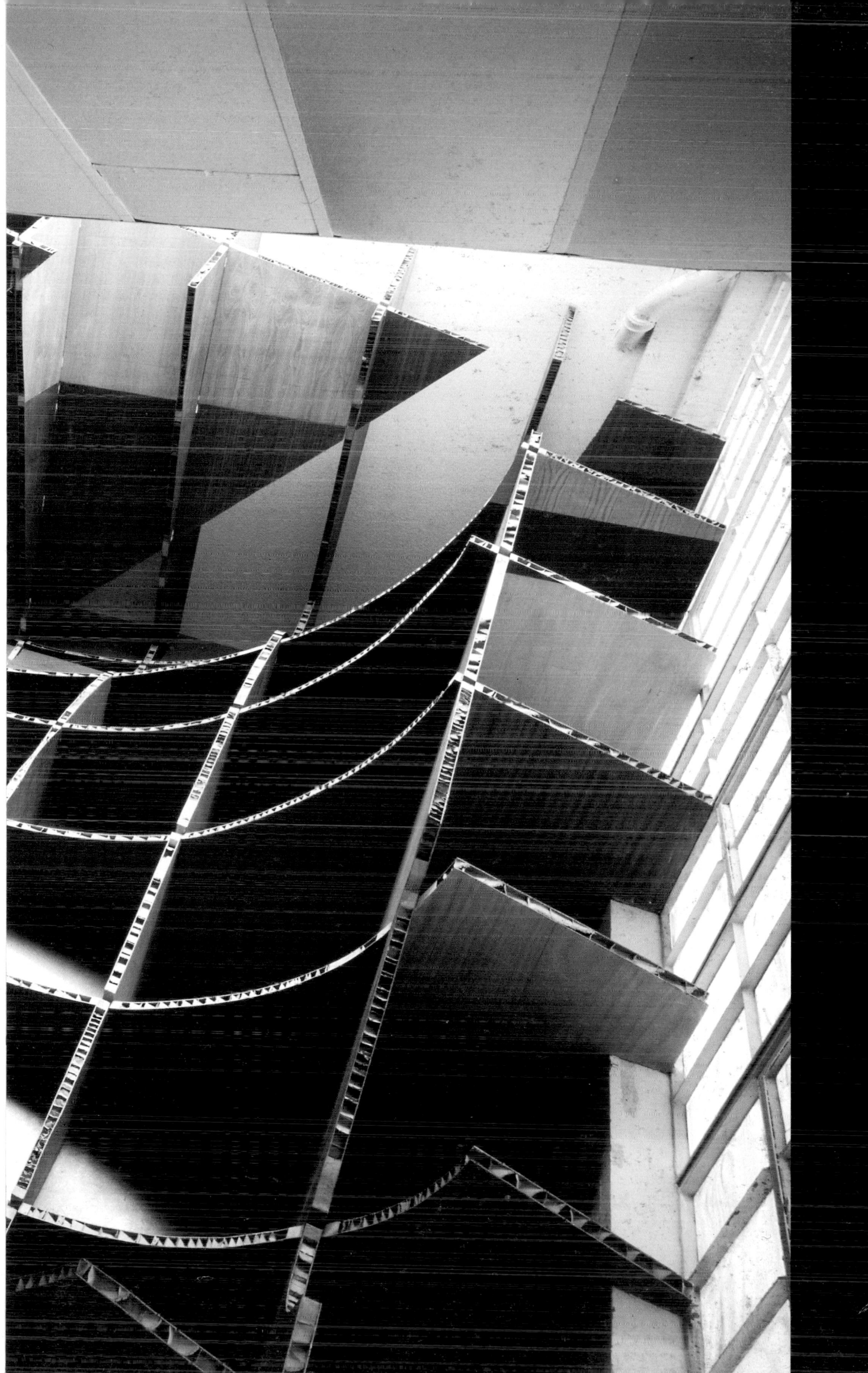

NAT GODDEN

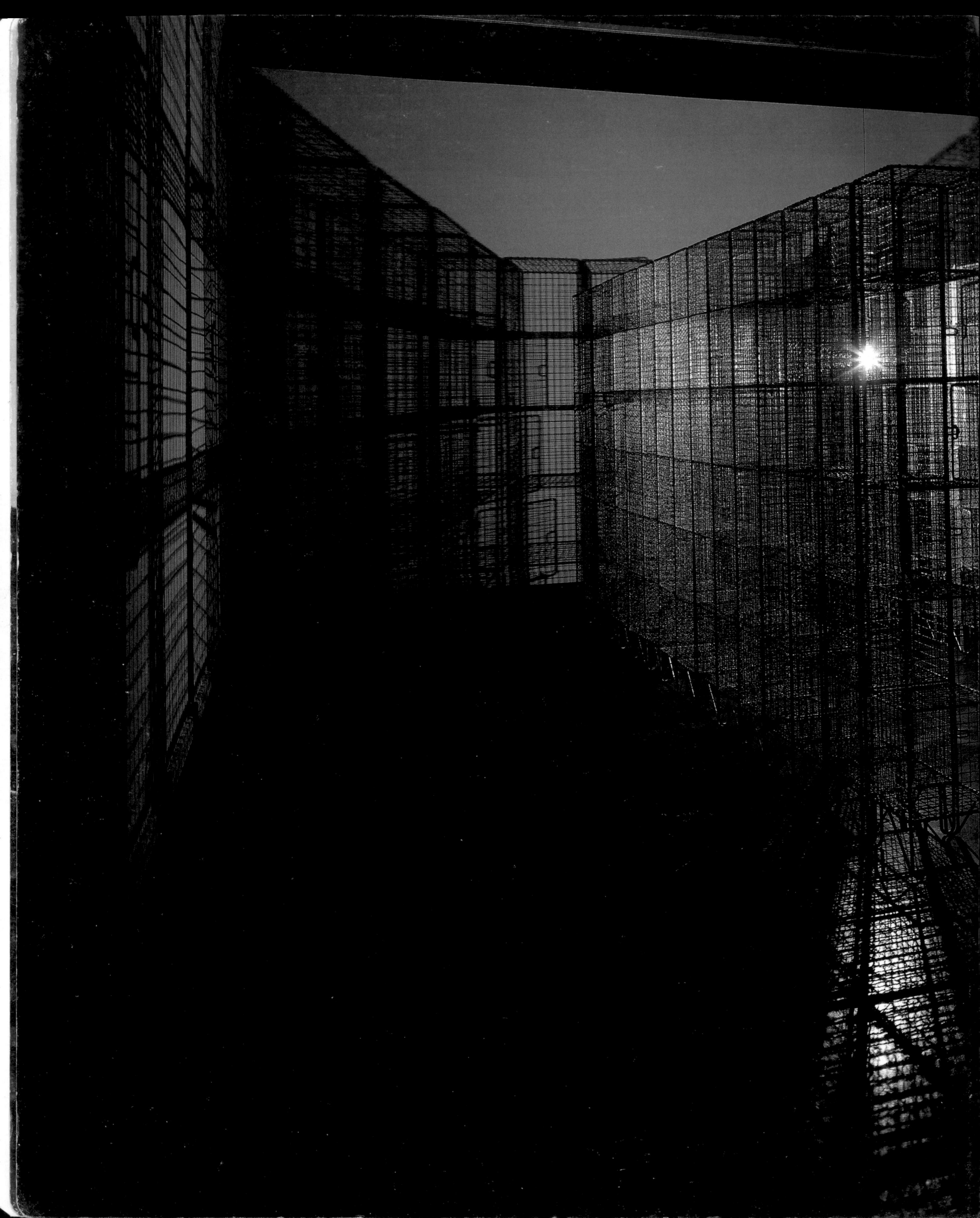

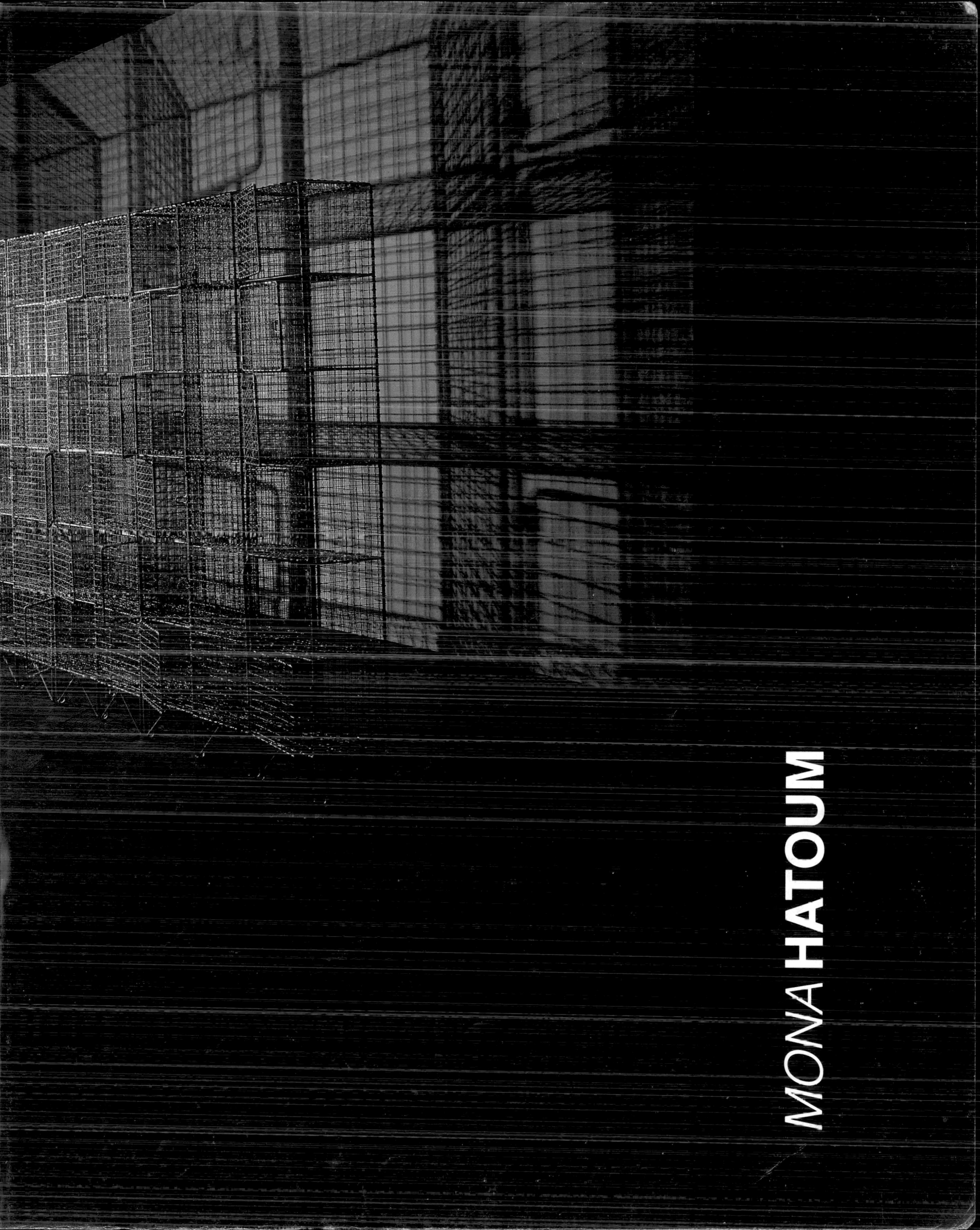

MONA HATOUM

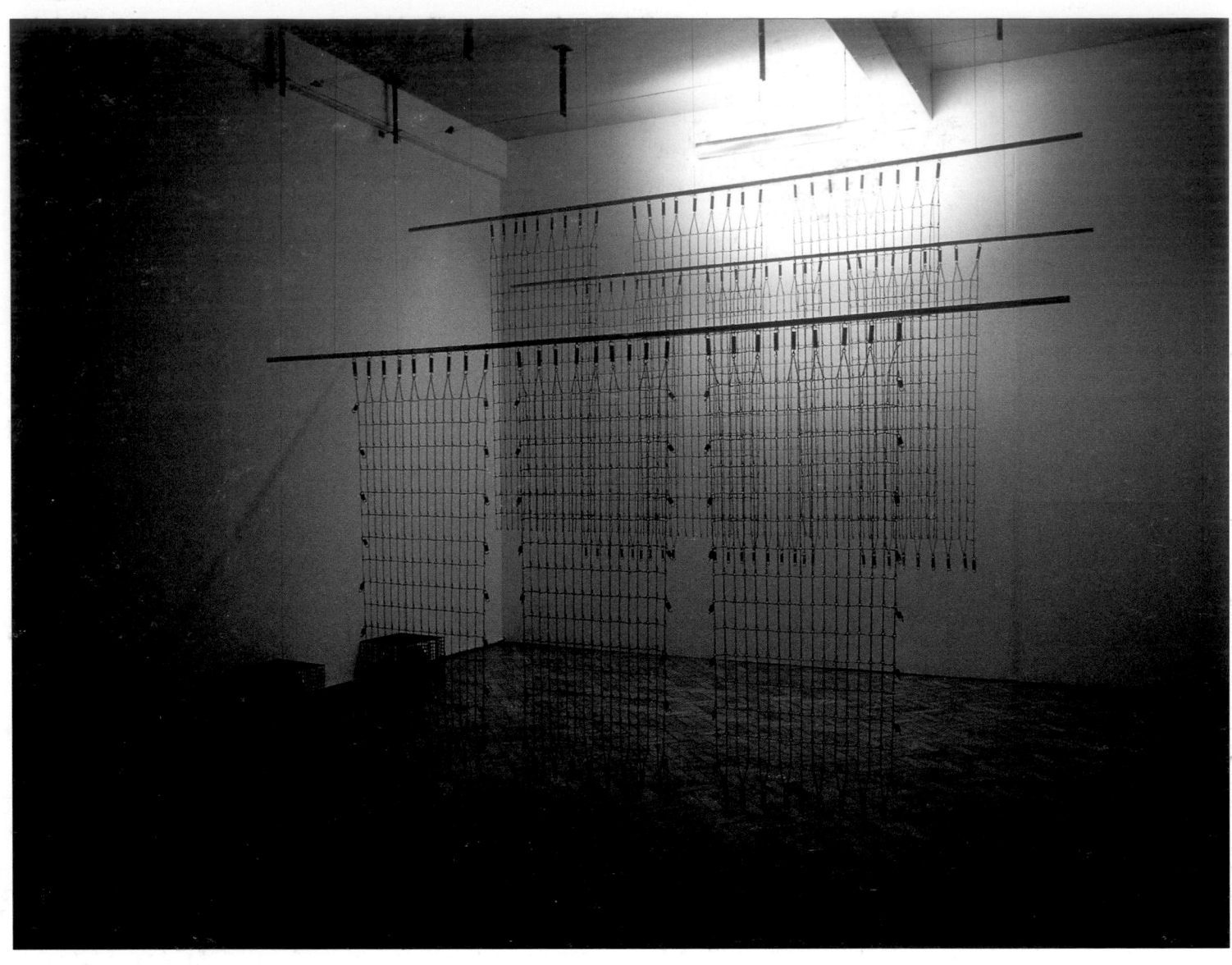

ABOVE
Short Space, *1992*
Installation at Chapter, Cardiff, 1992
Bed springs, electric motors, fluorescent strip
Dimensions: 5.45 x 5.10m

PREVIOUS PAGE
Light Sentence, *1992*
Installation at Chapter, Cardiff, 1992
Reconstructed for the Serpentine Gallery,
London, 1993
Wire mesh lockers, light bulb, electric motor
Dimensions: 1.98 x 1.85 x 5.18m

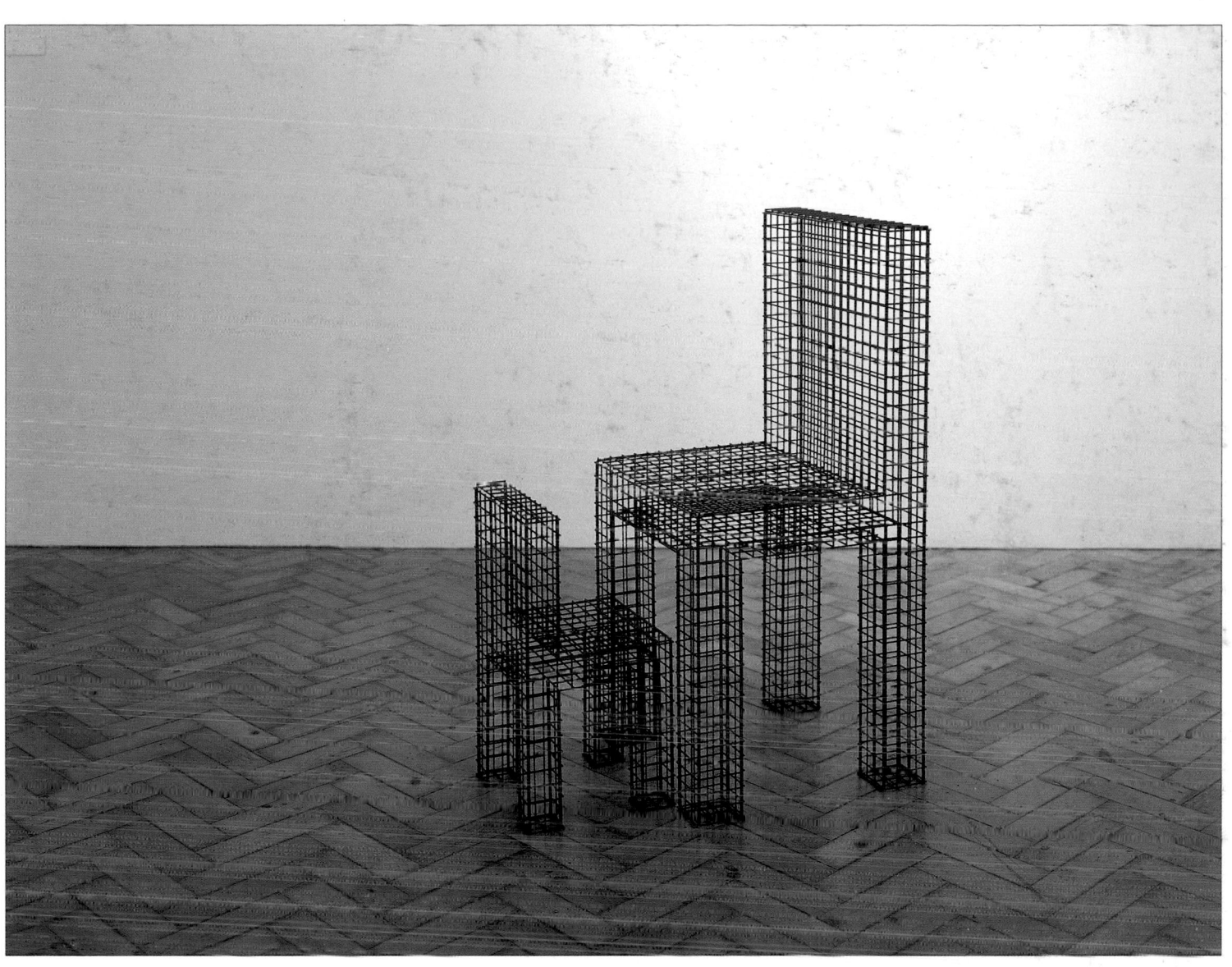

ABOVE
Untitled, *1992*
Wire mesh
Dimensions: 98 x 44 x 71cm

ABOVE AND OPPOSITE
Untitled, *1992*
Two views of installation at Mario Flecha
Gallery, London, 1992
Stainless steel wire
Dimensions of upper gallery: 9.0 x 4.0m
Dimensions of lower gallery: 5.0 x 5.0m

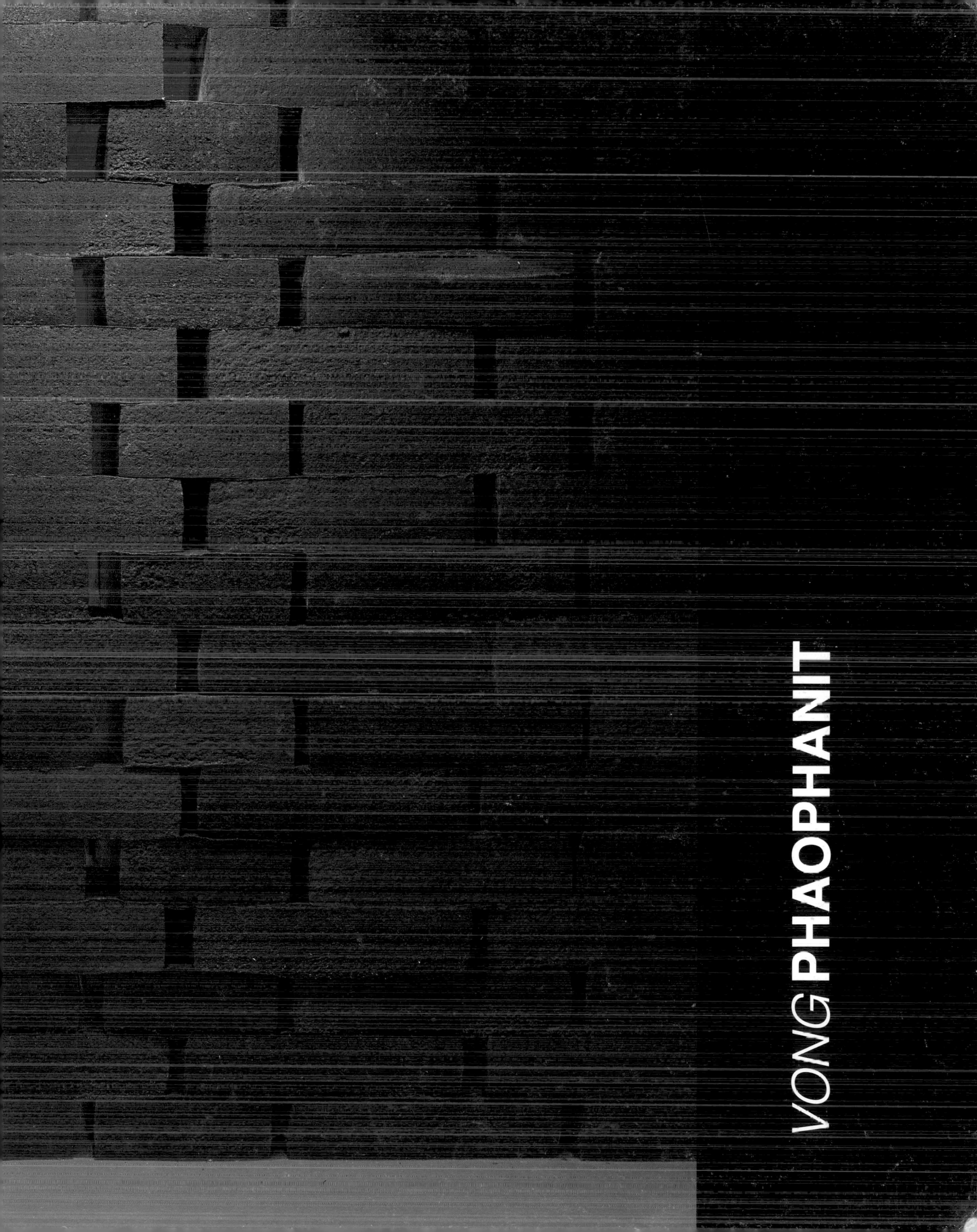

VONG PHAOPHANIT

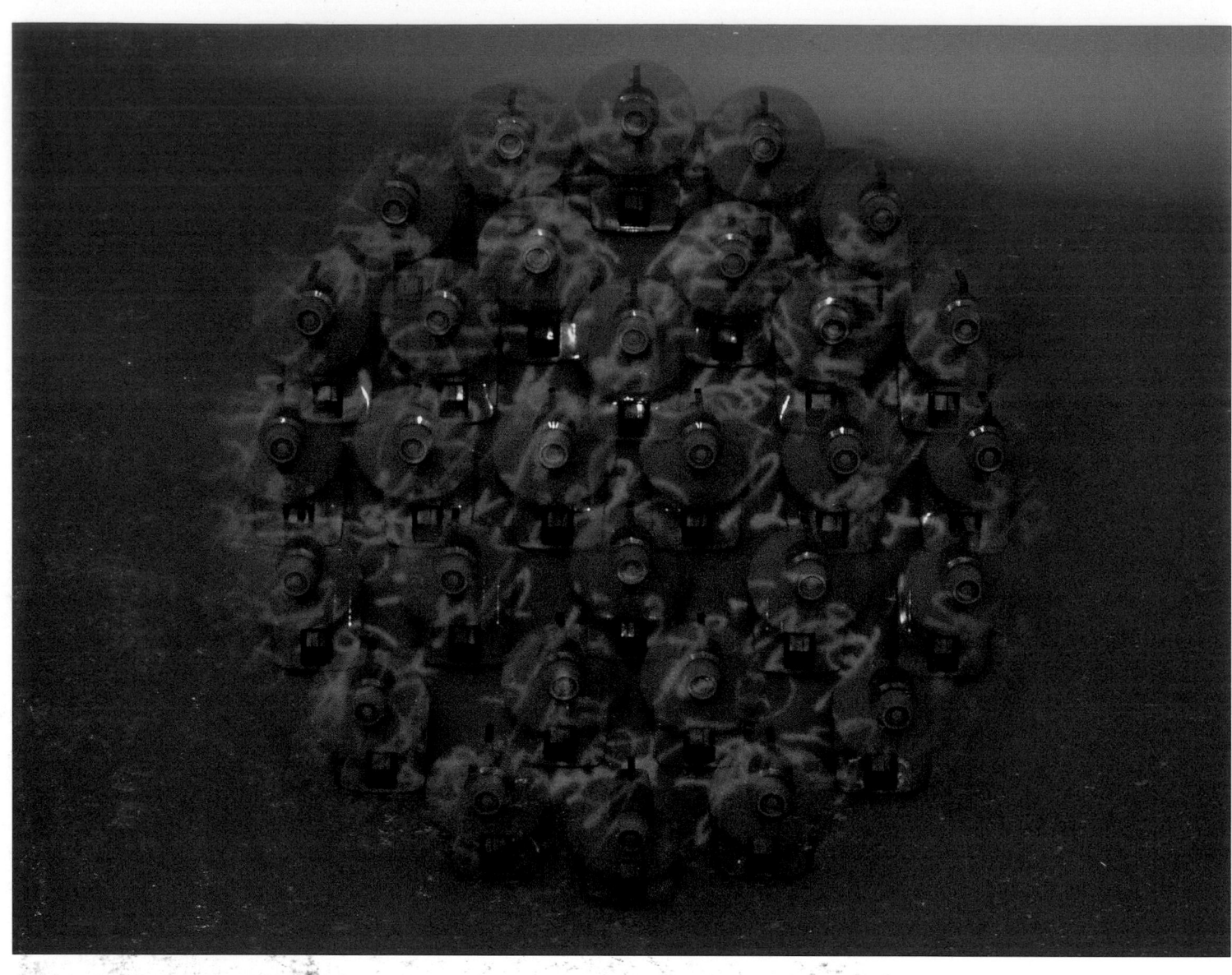

ABOVE
Fragments, *1990*
30 ventilator fans and slide projection
Diameter: 2.0m
Arts Council Collection

PREVIOUS PAGE
In the Shadow of Words, *1991*
Installation at Arnolfini, Bristol, 1991
Rubber brick wall and neon signs
Dimensions: 4.0 x 3.0m

ABOVE
Owls during the Day, Foxes at Night, *1990*
Installation in air-raid shelter for TSWA Four
Cities Project, Plymouth, 1990
Glass panels, rice, straw, neon
Dimensions of space: 15.0 x 27.0m

OVERLEAF
Neon Rice Field, *1993*
Installation at the Serpentine Gallery,
London, 1993
Neon, rice
Dimensions of gallery: 6.7 x 11.0m

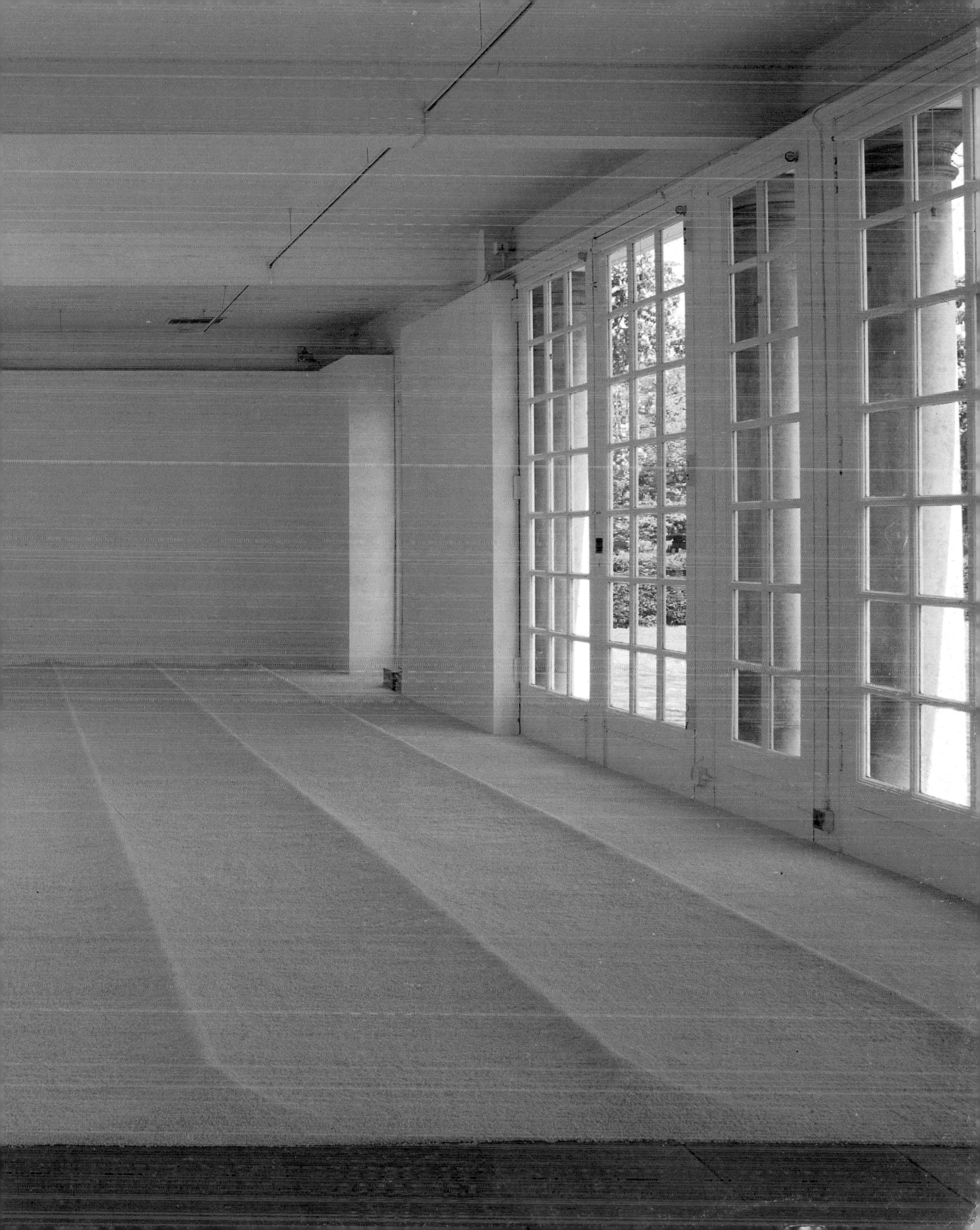

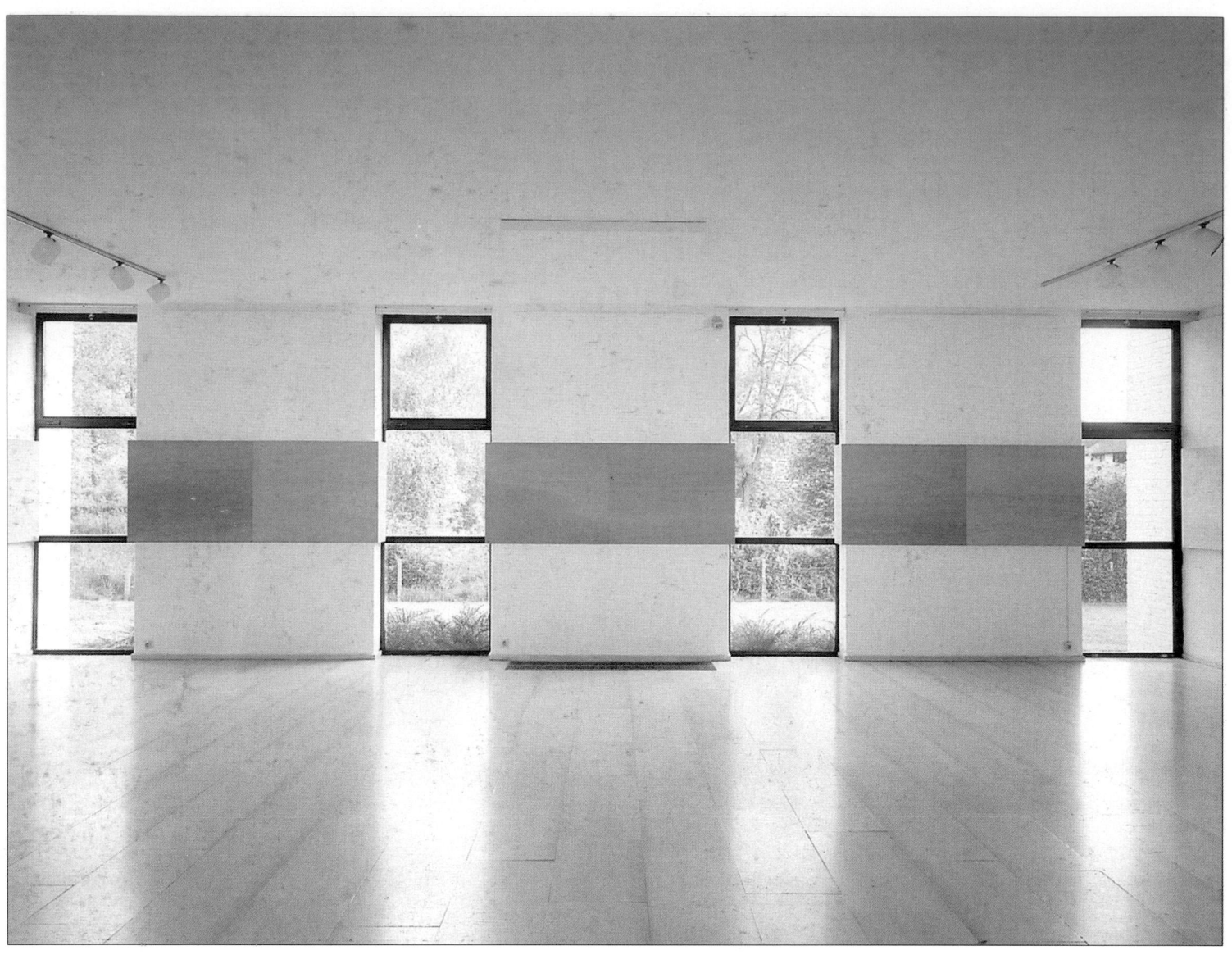

ABOVE
Wall-Meter-Surround, *1990*
Installation at Museum Dhondt-Dhaenens,
Deurle, 1990
Plywood
Dimensions of gallery: 3.5 x 12.0 x 9.0m

PREVIOUS PAGE
Wall-Meter-Plaster-Surround, *1992*
Installation at Laure Genillard Gallery,
London, 1992
Plaster, white paint
Dimensions of gallery: 3.0 x 4.0 x 7.0m

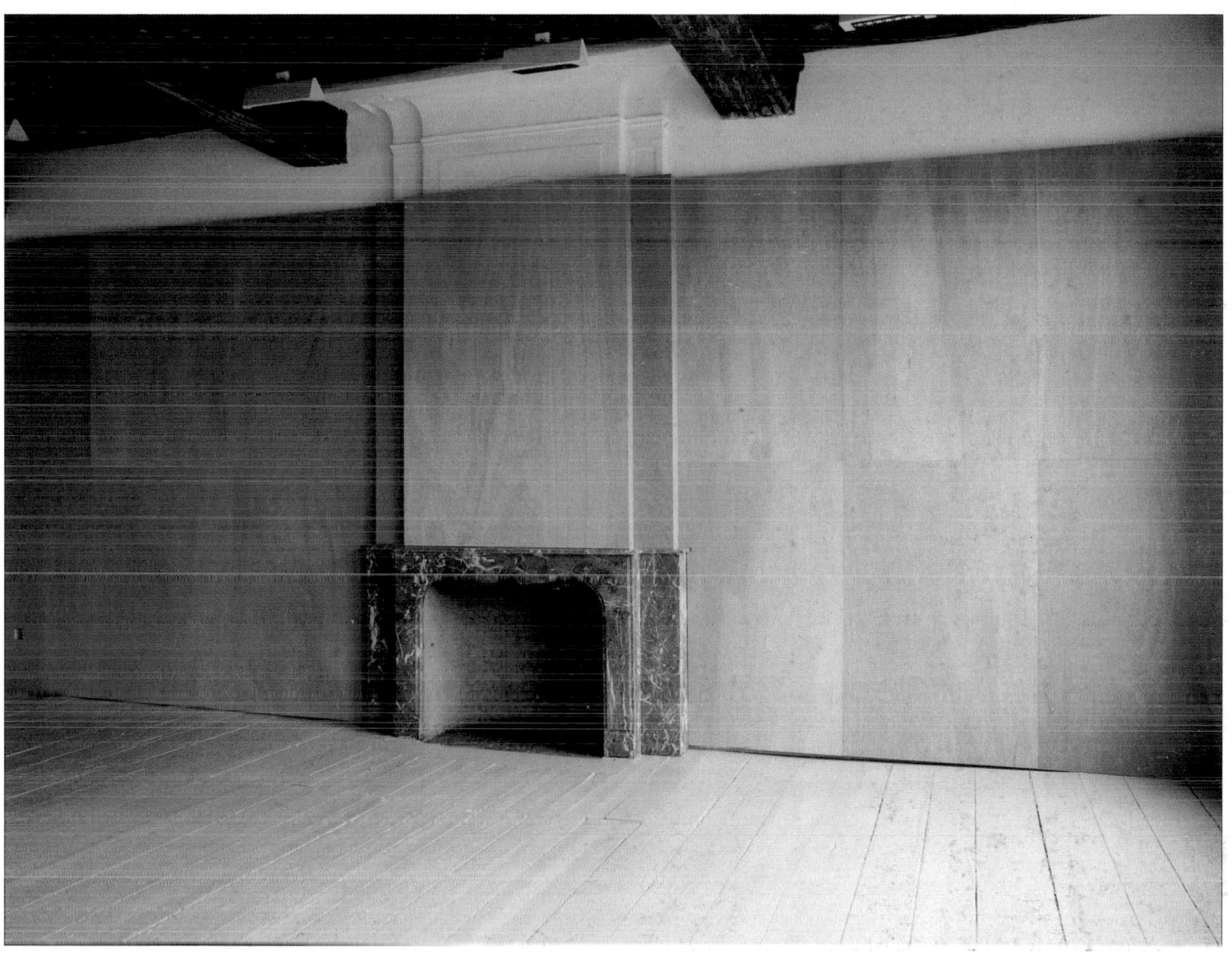

ABOVE
Untitled, 1991
Installation at Galerie Bruges La Morte,
Bruges, 1991
Plywood
Dimensions: 3.0 x 7.0m

OVERLEAF
Untitled, 1993
Installation at the Serpentine Gallery,
London, 1993
Plywood
Dimensions of gallery: 4.0 x 10.0 x 8.0m

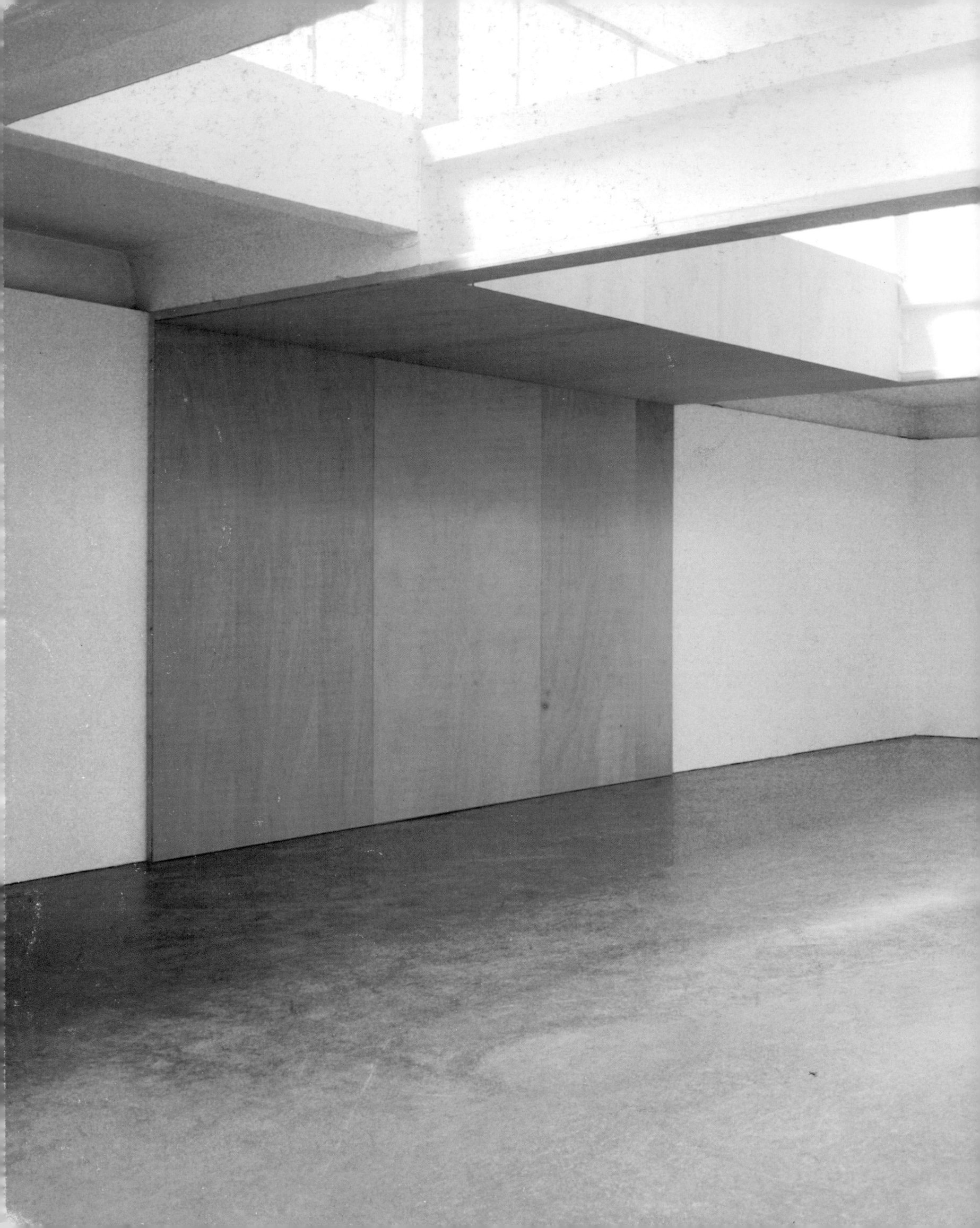

NAT GOODDEN

Born: 1947, Colchester

Education: 1965-66, North East Essex School of Art; 1966-69 St Martin's School of Art, London, BA Hons Sculpture

Solo Exhibitions:
1982   Matt's Gallery, London
        Spectro Gallery, Newcastle-upon-Tyne
1983   Akumulatory 2, Poznan, Poland
1990   Matt's Gallery, London

Group Exhibitions:
1974   Studio exhibition, London
1975   SPACE Open Studios, London
        AIR Gallery, London
1978   Studio exhibition, London

MONA HATOUM

Born: 1952, Beirut, Lebanon
Living in London since 1975

Education: 1970-72 Beirut University College, Beirut, Lebanon; 1975-79 The Byam Shaw School of Art, London; 1979-81 The Slade School of Art, London

1989-92 Senior Fellow at Cardiff Institute of Higher Education

Selected Solo Exhibitions:
1991   Oboro Gallery, Montreal
1992   'Dissected Space', Chapter, Cardiff
        Mario Flecha Gallery, London
1993   Arnolfini, Bristol

Selected Group Exhibitions:
1989   'The Light at the End', The Showroom, London
        'Intimate Distance', The Photographers' Gallery, London and national tour
        'The Other Story', Hayward Gallery, London
1990   'The British Art Show', McLellan Galleries, Glasgow; Leeds City Art Gallery; Hayward Gallery, London; TSWA Four Cities Project, Newcastle-upon-Tyne
1991   'Shocks to the System' Arts Council Collection, Royal Festival Hall, London; Northern Centre for Contemporary Art, Sunderland; Ikon Gallery, Birmingham; Chapter, Cardiff; Royal Albert Memorial Museum, Exeter; City

Museum and Art Gallery, Plymouth; Maclaurin Art Gallery, Ayr
        'Interrogating Identity', Grey Art Gallery, New York and US tour (-1993)
        'The Interrupted Life', The New Museum of Contemporary Art, New York
1992   'Pour la Suite du Monde', Musée d'art contemporain de Montreal, Canada

VONG PHAOPHANIT

Born: 1961, Savannakhet, Laos
Living in Britain since 1985

Education: 1980-85 Ecole des Beaux-Arts, Aix-en-Provence, France

Selected Solo Exhibitions:
1986   'Aqua Pittura', Espace Sextius, Aix-en-Provence
1987   'Just A Moment', 'Tea Ceremony', Spacex Gallery, Exeter
1988   'Just A Moment', 'Fragments', Chapter, Cardiff
1990   'In the shadow of words', Arnolfini, Bristol
        'Owls during the Day, Foxes at Night', TSWA Four Cities Project, Plymouth
1991   'tok tem dean kep kin bo dai (what falls to the ground but can't be eaten)', Chisenhale Gallery, London
1992   'tok tem dean kep kin bo dai (what falls to the ground but can't be eaten)', Ikon Gallery, Birmingham

Selected Group Exhibitions:
1987   'If Looks Could Kill', Red Herring Gallery, Brighton
        'Scaffolding Art Project', out-door site specific installation, Brighton
1989   'Fragments', out-door site specific installation, Amsterdam
        'The Artist Abroad', Usher Gallery, Lincoln; City Museum and Art Gallery, Plymouth
1990   'From Moment to Moment', Cambridge Darkroom, Cambridge
        'Fragments', 'The British Art Show', McLellan Galleries, Glasgow; Leeds City Art Gallery; Hayward Gallery, London
        'In the Shadow of Words', Bergen Kunstforening, Bergen

1991   'Fragments', 'Shocks to the System', Arts Council Collection: Royal Festival Hall, London; Northern Centre for Contemporary Art, Sunderland; Ikon Gallery, Birmingham; Chapter, Cardiff; Royal Albert Memorial Museum, Exeter; City Museum and Art Gallery, Plymouth; Maclaurin Art Gallery, Ayr
1992   'Multiplici Culture', Rome
1993   'Prospect 93', Frankfurter Kunsteverein, Frankfurt
        'Aperto 93', Venice Biennale
        Thames Barrier Project, Greenwich, London

Awards:
1991   GWS Mellhuish Fine Art Fellowship

GLADSTONE THOMPSON

Born: 1959, London

Education: 1984-87 Chelsea School of Art, London, BA Hons Fine Art; 1987-89 Atelier 63, Haarlem, The Netherlands

Solo Exhibitions:
1989   Laure Genillard Gallery, London
1992   Galerie des Archives, Paris
        Laure Genillard Gallery, London
1993   Cairn Gallery, Nailsworth, Gloucestershire (with Lesley Foxcroft)

Group Exhibitions:
1987   Riverside Studios Open Exhibition, London
1990   Museum Dhondt-Dhaenens, Deurle
1991   Galerie Bruges La Morte, Bruges
        'Present Continuous', Bath Festival Exhibition
        'Spoleto Artedomani 1991', Spoleto
1992   'Human Properties', Ikon Gallery, Birmingham
        '30-11', Galerie des Archives, Paris
        'Etats Specifiques', Musée des Beaux-Arts André Malraux, Le Havre
        Galerie des Archives, Paris
1993   Burnett Miller Gallery, Los Angeles

INSTALLATION ART

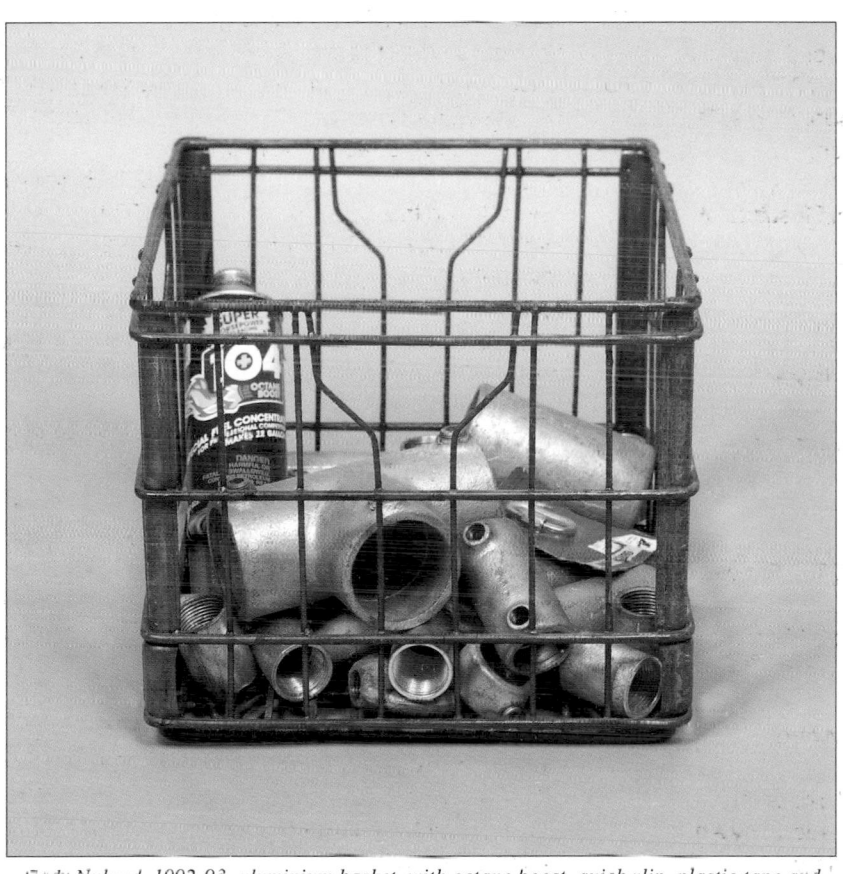

Cady Noland, 1992–93, aluminium basket, with octane boost, quick clip, plastic tape and metal fittings (photo: Geoffrey Clements)

Acknowledgements

We would above all like to thank Andrew Benjamin for his help in putting together this issue of *Art & Design*, we would also like to thank all the artists, writers and galleries who so generously provided us with material. *Half Title* the artist; *Frontis* Anthony d'Offay, London; *Title* Guggenheim Museum, New York; *Contents* Lisson Gallery, London; **On Installation** *pp6-23* all material courtesy of the co-directors of the Museum of Installation, London, we are especially grateful to Michael Petry for his time; **Ex Situ** *pp24-30* essay translated by Vivian Constantinopoulos, *p24* Lisson Gallery, London; **Matter and Meaning of Installation** *pp31-33 p33* Philadelphia Museum of Art, Louise and Walter Arensberg Collections; **Gordon Matta-Clark** *pp34-41* images and quotations from *Gordon Matta-Clark*, exhib cat, IVAM, Valencia, 1992; **Interview with James Turrell** *pp42-51* We are grateful to Susan Brades of the Hayward Gallery, London for her help, images courtesy Anthony d'Offay Gallery; **Reserves of Spatial Events** *pp52-57* essay translated by Anne Boyman, first published in *Constructing the Perceiver – Arakawa: Experimental Works*, National Museum of Modern Art, Tokyo, 1991, *p52* courtesy the artist; **Landing Sites/The End of Spacetime** *pp58-79* all images courtesy Arakawa and Madeline Gins; **Richard Artschwager** *pp80-81* all images Public/Private, New York; **Donald Judd** *pp82-83* statement extracted from Donald Judd *On Installation*, 1982, images courtesy the artist; **Cady Noland** *pp84-85* images courtesy the artist; **Anya Gallaccio** *pp86-87* text extract from interview with Kim Sweet, 1992, ICA, images Karsten Schubert London; **Andrew Sabin** *pp88-89* images courtesy the artist; **Wolfgang Laib** *pp90-91* text extract from interview by Martin Schwander, 1990, images Sperone Westwater, New York; **Judith Barry** *pp92-93* Fondation pour l'Architecture, Brussels; **Joseph Kosuth** *pp94-96* all images courtesy the artist

COVER: Arakawa and Madeline Gins, Site of Reversible Destiny, *1978- present, detail*
INSIDE FRONT COVER: Richard Artschwager, blps, *Galerie Konrad Fischer, Düsseldorf, 1968*
INSIDE BACK COVER: Joseph Kosuth, Passagen-Werk *(Documenta Flânerie), June-September 1992, Documenta IX, Kassel*

HOUSE EDITOR: Nicola Hodges EDITORIAL TEAM: Ramona Khambatta, Katherine MacInnes
SENIOR DESIGNER: Andrea Bettella DESIGN CO-ORDINATOR: Mario Bettella DESIGN TEAM: Jacqueline Grosvenor, Gregory Mills

First published in Great Britain in 1993 by *Art & Design*
Second impression May 1996, an imprint of
ACADEMY GROUP LTD, 42 LEINSTER GARDENS, LONDON W2 3AN
Member of the VCH Publishing Group

ISBN: 1 85490 213 X

Distributed to the trade in the United States of America by
NATIONAL BOOK NETWORK, INC, 4720 BOSTON WAY, LANHAM, MARYLAND 20706

Printed and bound in Singapore

Contents

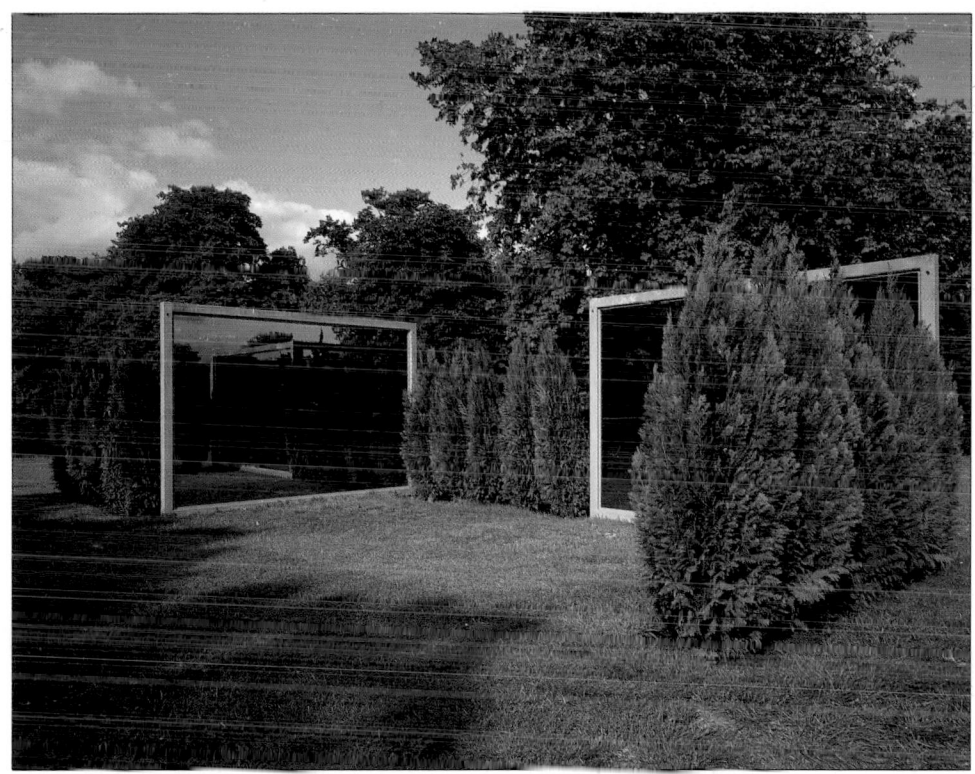

Dan Graham, Two-way Mirror and Hedge Labyrinth, *1989, zinc sprayed steel, two way mirror, clear glass and blue cypress trees, installed at the Serpentine Gallery, London, 1992 (photo: Steven White)*

ART & DESIGN PROFILE No 30

INSTALLATION ART

Guest-Edited by Andrew Benjamin

Nicolas de Oliveira, Nicola Oxley and Michael Petry On Installation 6

Thierry de Duve Ex Situ 24

Andrew Benjamin Matter and Meaning: On Installations 31

Corinne Diserens Gordon Matta-Clark 34

Clare Farrow An Interview with James Turrell 42

Jean-François Lyotard Reserves of Spatial Events: Arakawa and Madeline Gins 52

Arakawa and Madeline Gins Landing Sites/The End of Spacetime 58

Richard Artschwager 80; Donald Judd 82; Cady Noland The Mirror Device 84

Anya Gallaccio 86; Andrew Sabin The Sea of Sun 88

Wolfgang Laib 90; Judith Barry 92

Joseph Kosuth 94

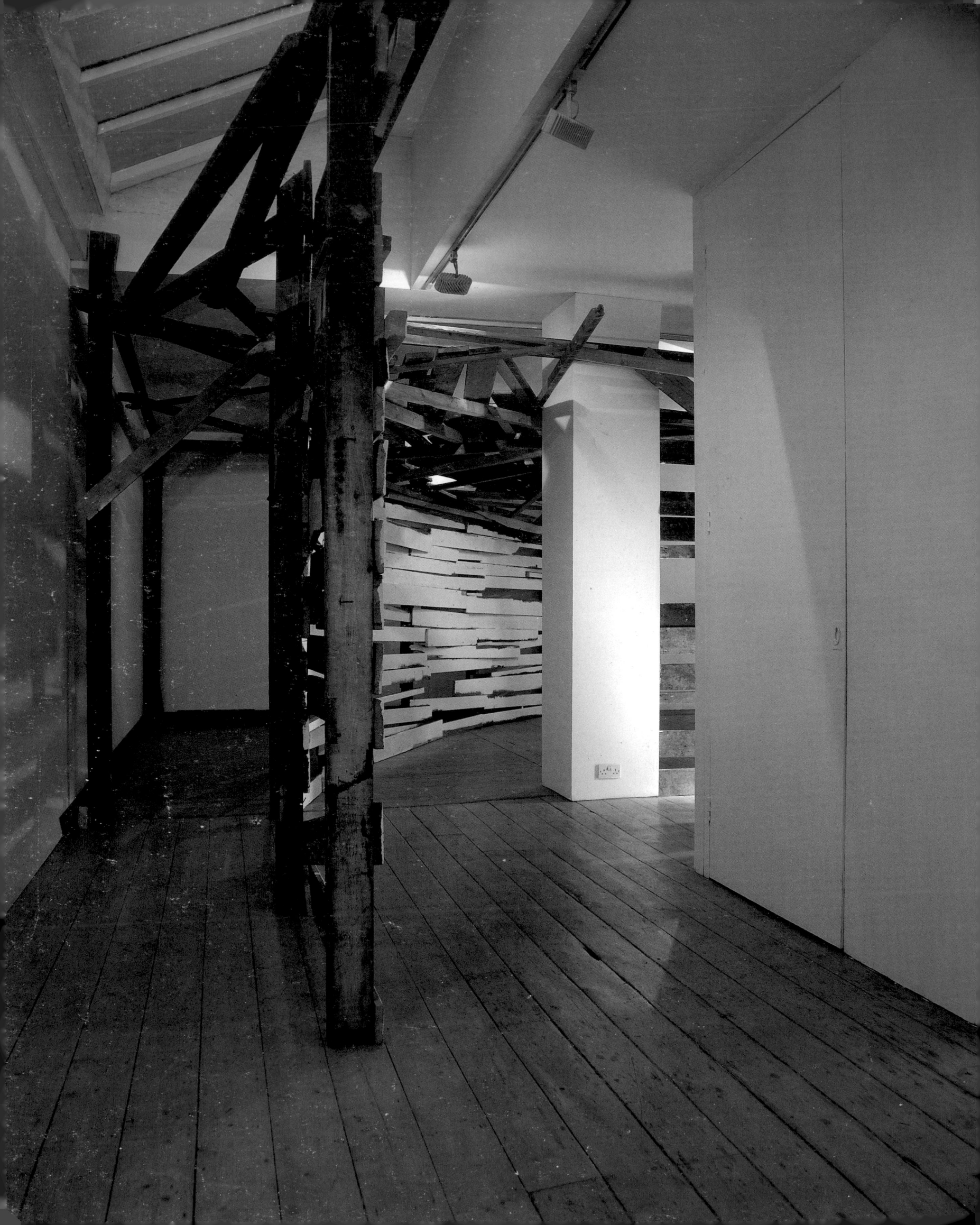

NICOLAS DE OLIVEIRA, NICOLA OXLEY AND MICHAEL PETRY
ON INSTALLATION

The term 'installation' has established itself firmly as a part of the vocabulary of the visual arts. Many artists and critics have refered to the activity as an expression of the concept of *Gesammtkunstwerk*, a total work of art, as it appears to borrow from a vast spectrum of disciplines. Its history, while often ill defined, grows out of the individual narratives presented by architecture, painting, sculpture, theatre and performance. It comes as no surprise that, even in its contemporary manifestation, installation continues to express its former allegiances. The practice is therefore defined by its 'hybrid' quality, concentrating diverse, even contradictory notions within its influence.

Without wishing to delve into a historical analysis, it is important to acknowledge the debt owed, not only to artforms, but also to specific movements, among which Constructivism, Dada, Surrealism, Pop Art, Concept Art and Land Art take particular prominence. The Suprematist, El Lissitzky created what is arguably the first installation, the *Proun Environment* in 1923. He alluded to the notion of space as a physical material with properties such as wood or stone. Space could therefore be turned into a form, a legacy still clearly visible in contemporary installations.

The concept of 'site-specificity' appears to underpin many current works, and can be traced back to the activities of 'Land Art' from the 60s onwards. Contemporary makers of installation however, tend to work primarily within an urban, historical and social context, rather than showing concern for the idealised notions of nature expounded by the earlier 'Earthworks'. In some installations by Joseph Kosuth, Tadashi Kawamata, and Per Barclay, the environment playing host to the work often originates the piece and forms a mutually dependent relationship. Installation is, in this respect, like other artforms, occupying territory traditionally seen as being outside the visual arts.

Early forms of theatre took place against the backdrop of the city and were clearly part of the urban fabric in an attitude where life became art and art became life. Installation continues to borrow from this tradition, not only by placing itself within a real rather than imaginary context, but also by appearing to replicate life.

Edward Kienholz's *Beanery*, Claes Oldenburg's *Roxy* and Jannis Kounellis' *Cavalli* all originated In the 1960s and while taking essentially different viewpoints, these, as well as Paul Thek's works, can be seen as direct precursors to the 'tableaux' of Guillaume Bijl in the 1980s and 90s. These assemblages of everyday life are reconstituted within the gallery and while their form remains, their functions and ultimately their meanings are stripped. The alienation of the viewer from life itself is intensified by the perfect simulation afforded by installation. The concept of the total artwork mentioned above finds a further application through the function of the spectacle. The spectacle often focuses on the monumentality of possible experience by the public, but also functions as a vehicle for the ritual. Public spectacles, as carriers of ritualised signs and meanings underpin human activity. The dual focus rests both on the installation as it embraces the senses, and on the participation of the spectator. The term 'looking' is superceded in installation by the concept of 'spectating', which assumes a higher involvement by the audience.

The *Honeymoon Project* by Miralda, in which the artist 'married' the Statue of Liberty to the Statue of Christopher Columbus, was preceded by elaborate public manufacture and display of the 'couple's' nuptual finery. SITE's *Highway 86 Processional* at the World Expo in Vancouver featured a lifesize grey painted highway, complete with vehicles that visitors walked on, as it wound down the main street into the water. Christo's installations and interventions also inhabit the city and the landscape in spectacular ways. The end-products of projects such as *Running Fence* and most recently the *Umbrellas Project* are monumental in scale and impact. Employing many hundreds of participants these vast structures are designed to have only a brief life-span. The process of the projects from their inception to their demise is crucial and may take years to unravel. Meticulous documentation is prepared at each stage, from concept drawings and texts to photographs and videos. The attempt to capture a three-dimensional work is complex enough, further complicated by the necessity to record the element of time. The document shows only fragments of the complete unit, yet the whole remains greater than the sum of its parts. The experience essentially provides the only way to create a summative view of the installation.

Time-based media such as live action, film and video technology, play an active role in the make-up of contemporary installation. These areas facilitate an access to narrative, as well as duration based events. When artists such as Bill Viola, Gary Hill and

OPPOSITE: Tadashi Kawamata, Installation at Annely Juda Fine Art, *1990*

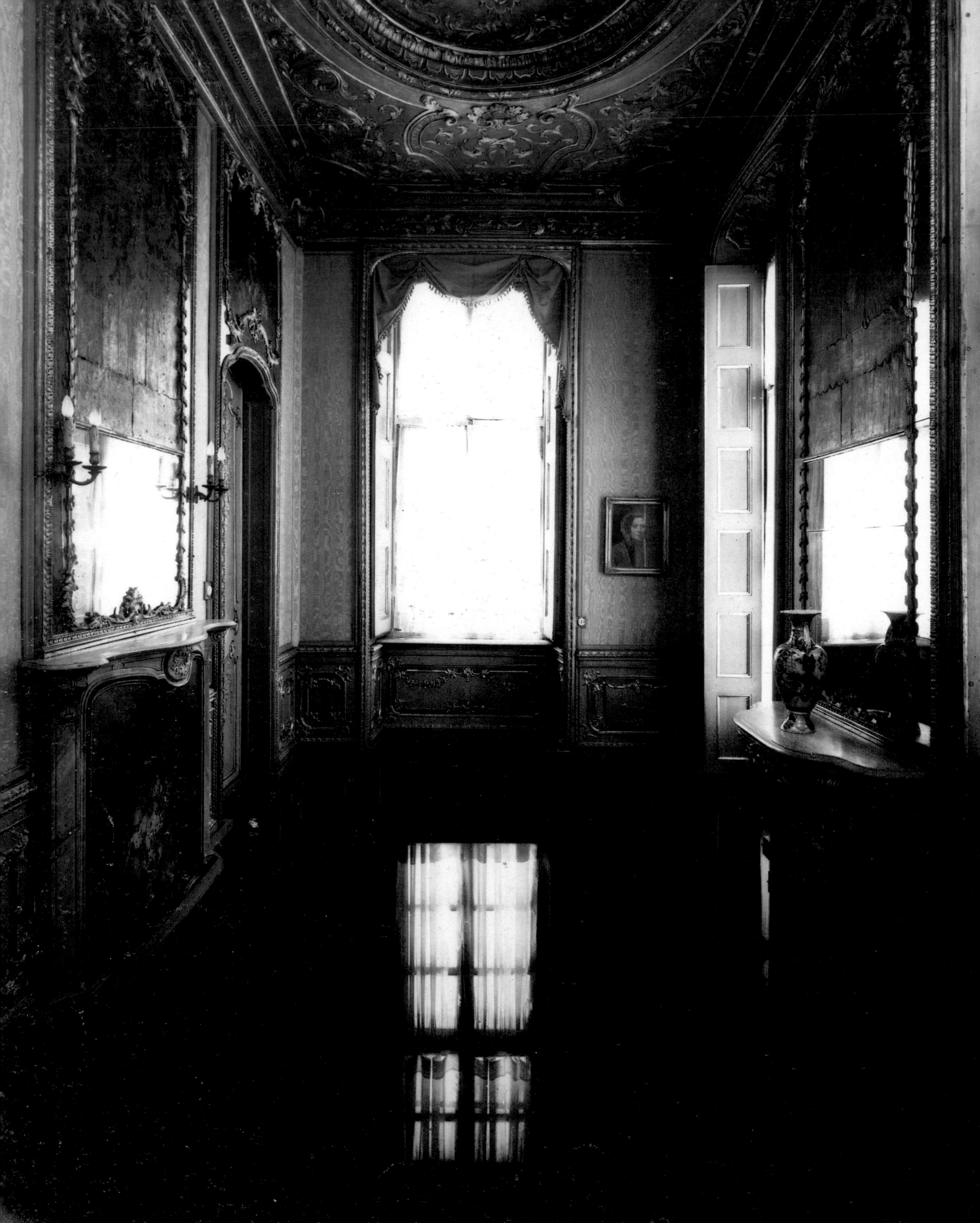

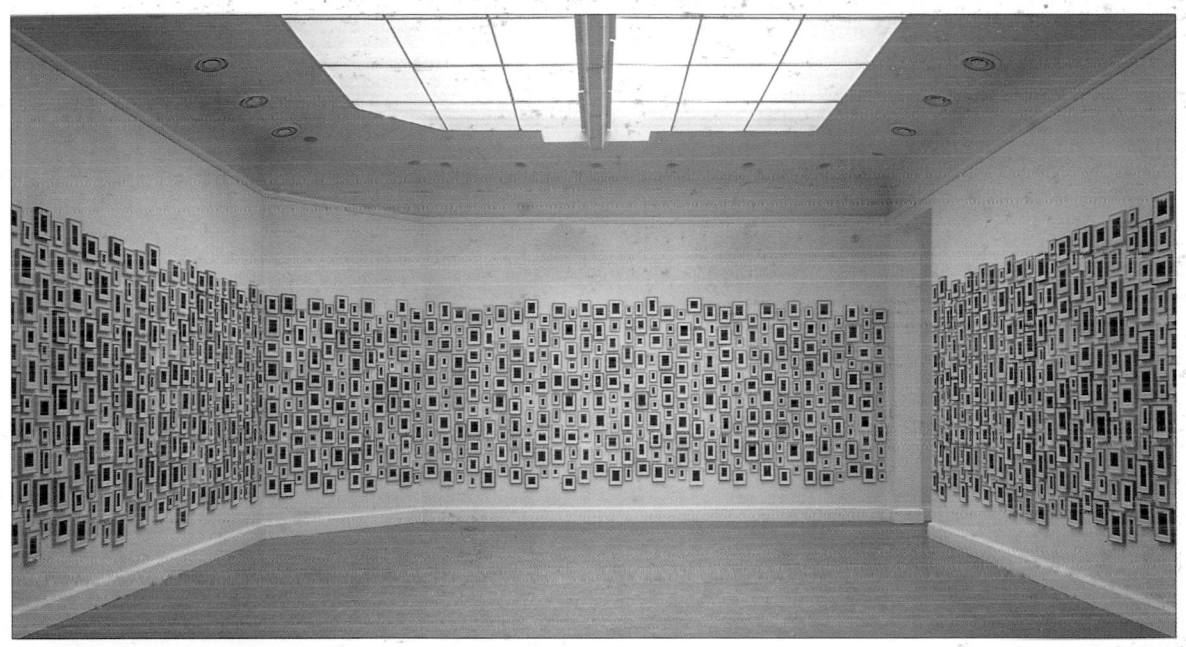

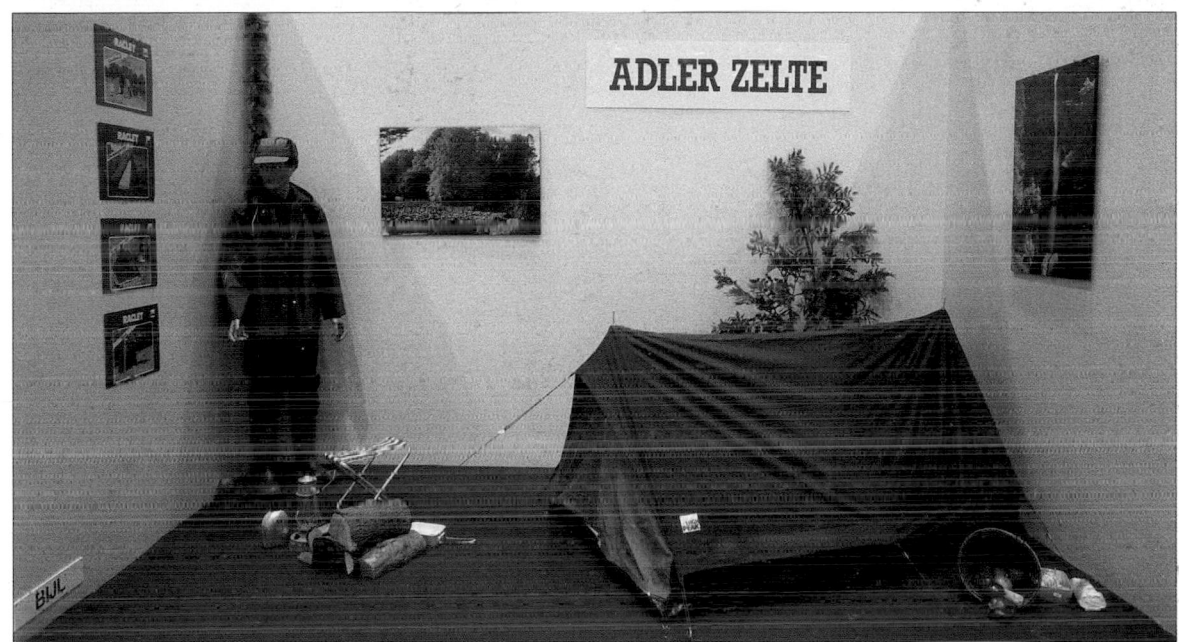

ADLER ZELTE

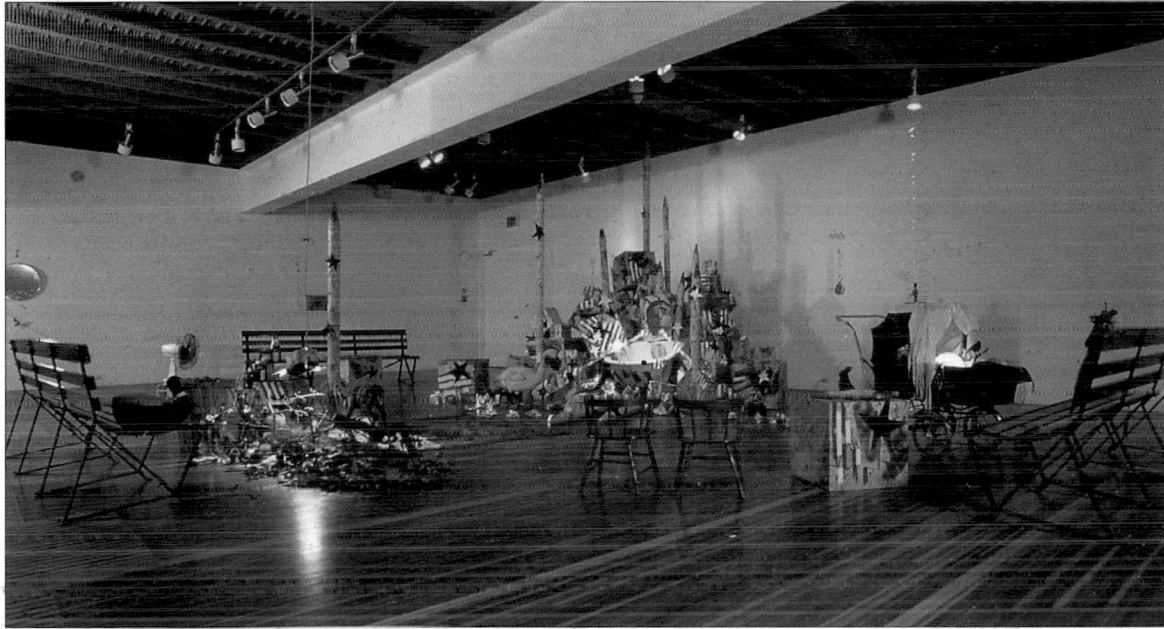

ABOVE: Allan McCollum, Perfect Vehicles, (1985) 1989; CENTRE: Guillaume Bijl, Adler Zelte, Cologne; BELOW: Paul Thek, Missiles and Bunnies, Hirshhorn, Washington DC, 1984; OPPOSITE: Per Barclay, The Chinese Room, 1990, installation with motor oil, Palazzo Barolo, Turin (photo: Paolo Pellion)

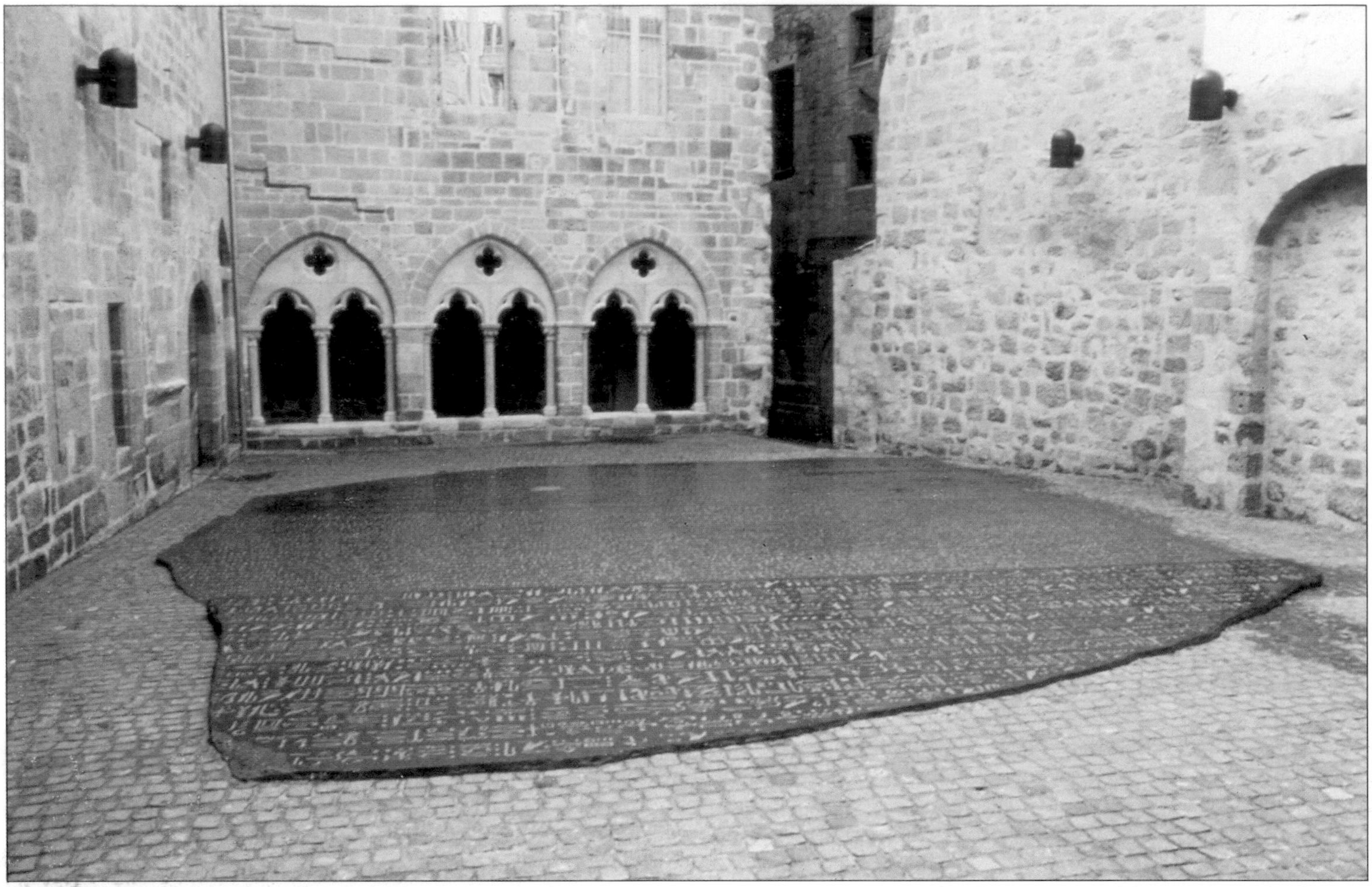

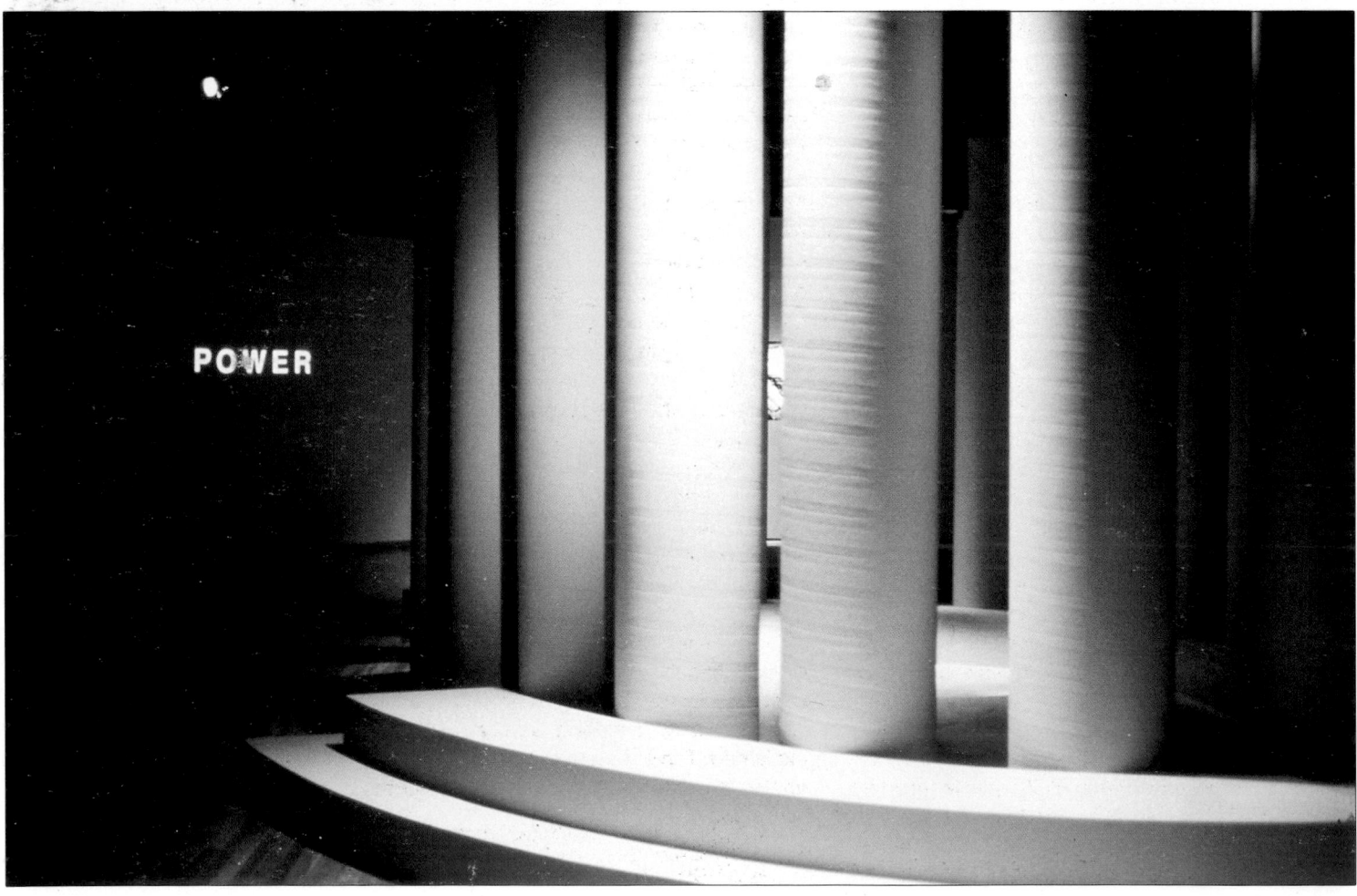

Dara Birnbaum presented their installations at the 1992 Documenta in Kassel, they clearly addressed the narrative potential of the media at their disposal. The spectator becomes an integral part of the work by virtue of the duration of a common experience. Muntadas' *Stadium* dealt with the relationship of power between the media and the masses using film, slides and a built environment.

If much of current installation practice appears to inhabit specific, physical spaces, it does so often unbounded by the architectural container. The work may essentially exist within the given space, yet this has not precluded artists from transporting their audiences out of the surroundings into imagined places. Brodsky and Utkins' untitled work at the Tacoma Arts Museum in 1990 created an internal architectural space, made from alabaster moulds and debris. The experience of being here, yet simultaneously occupying a different realm, is well known to the spectator. Christian Boltanski's *Missing House* is an indictment of the atrocities inflicted upon the Jewish population under the Nazi-regime in Germany that took place on a site which had been razed to the ground during the war. His intervention, while stating the lack or the disappearence of the building successfully projected upon it by interrence an imagined space, the spectre of the past.

The issues of culture and history have been addressed by many installations within the institutional framework, aided by the fact that major museums have begun to commission temporary works. Museums of Science, Art and Ethnography are important vehicles for the shaping of culture, acting as recipients and 'curators' of the past. The museum's role as guardian of 'timeless' works appears perhaps hostile to works which are essentially temporal, but recent installations have been instrumental in tackling the necessity of formulating a new role for the institutions. Works at the Carnegie International in 1992 by artists such as Barbara Bloom and Sophie Calle used the context of the institution and drew extensively on exhibits from its collection. Through the deployment of the 'found object' and the use of the museum's structures the installations offered a dissenting voice. The open-ended project has come to represent one of the main avenues for installation, recapturing an ambivalent and experimental edge.

Large-scale thematic exhibitions have also offered artists specific locations and cultural contexts from which to work. These interventions vary from the spectacular environment to the slightest of interferences. At the Berlin exhibition *Die Endlichkeit Der Freiheit* (The Finiteness of Freedom) in 1990, Ilya Kabakov placed a monumental work comprising two sets of wooden parallel walls on the site of the demolished Berlin Wall, while Mario Merz placed two discreet neon signs which read 'Why' above the tracks in a railway station. Both artists addressed the context, and the momentous

changes of the German re-unification while sharing neither scale nor form. Whether constructed by the artist, or in place a priori, the context for the work constitutes an important focus for the artist – one which to a large extent dictates the scale of the intervention.

The obstacles presented by different spaces have lead artists to adapt works of a single title to a range of places. Allan McCollum's *Perfect Vehicles (1985) 1989* takes the form of a myriad of small plaster cast surrogates of framed artworks with the place for an image painted out, and have been reinstalled in a variety of guises worldwide. Richard Wilson's *20/50*, originally sited at Matts Gallery London was remade for the Scottish National Gallery and purchased by Saatchi for his collection. The apparent shift is less concerned with the artist's integrity or rigour, but relies on the open-ended nature of the activity. The difference between 'Installation' and 'Installed Work' diminishes when one is reminded of the fact that pure form is not what defines the discipline. Moreover, the other clear application of a definition, that of style, is of little use when creating boundaries. Installation is bounded, not so much by diversity of spaces, works and attitudes but by actual difference. Through the act of embracing a multiplicity of artforms, media, cultures and histories, it necessarily inherits the differences and discordances between them. Space, place and time, may be addressed as fictional constructs in work, yet ultimately they represent tangible experiences. When El Lissitzky claimed space (and by implication, time) as an artform for his *Environments*, he may have seen that this very space was already claimed by everyday life. The problematic in attempting to define installation rests with the application of inadequate terms. To summarise the practice as a series of clearly proscribed actions would be akin to describing painting as something which is performed with brushes on flat surfaces. As artists cross over into different media, the parts of the installation are not necessarily assessed by the criteria operating within those disciplines.

Installation essentially relies on a multiplicity of forms and attitudes leading to projects which positively make use of 'process' to reaffirm and 'problematise' their open-endedness manifest in complex contextuality and shifting temporality. Installation Art is its parts in relation to each other but is experienced as a whole. Installation Art is greater than the sum of its parts. Installation Art is based in the aesthetic experience that in the end cannot be fully described, depicted, recorded or explained. The spectator, who in the act of experiencing the work, acts as catalyst and receptor.

The authors of this piece, the Co-Directors of the Museum of Installation, London, are producing a volume on Installation Art with Thames & Hudson in December 1993

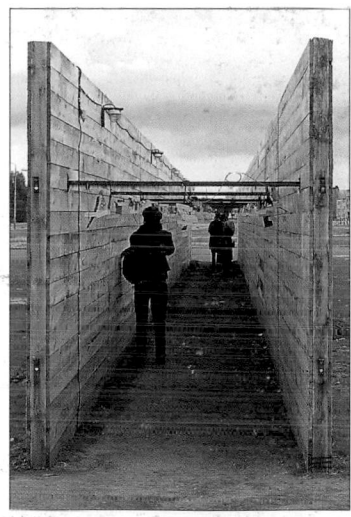

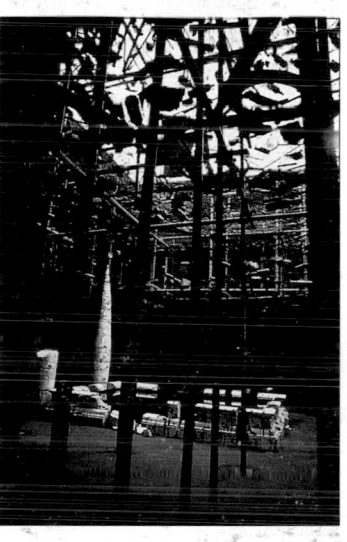

ABOVE: Ilya Kabakov, Berlin, 1990; BELOW: Brodsky and Utkin, Untitled, Tacoma Art Museum, between spring and summer 1990; OPPOSITE ABOVE: Joseph Kosuth, Ex Libris – JF Champollion (Figeac), 1991; OPPOSITE BELOW: Muntadas, Stadium, 1989

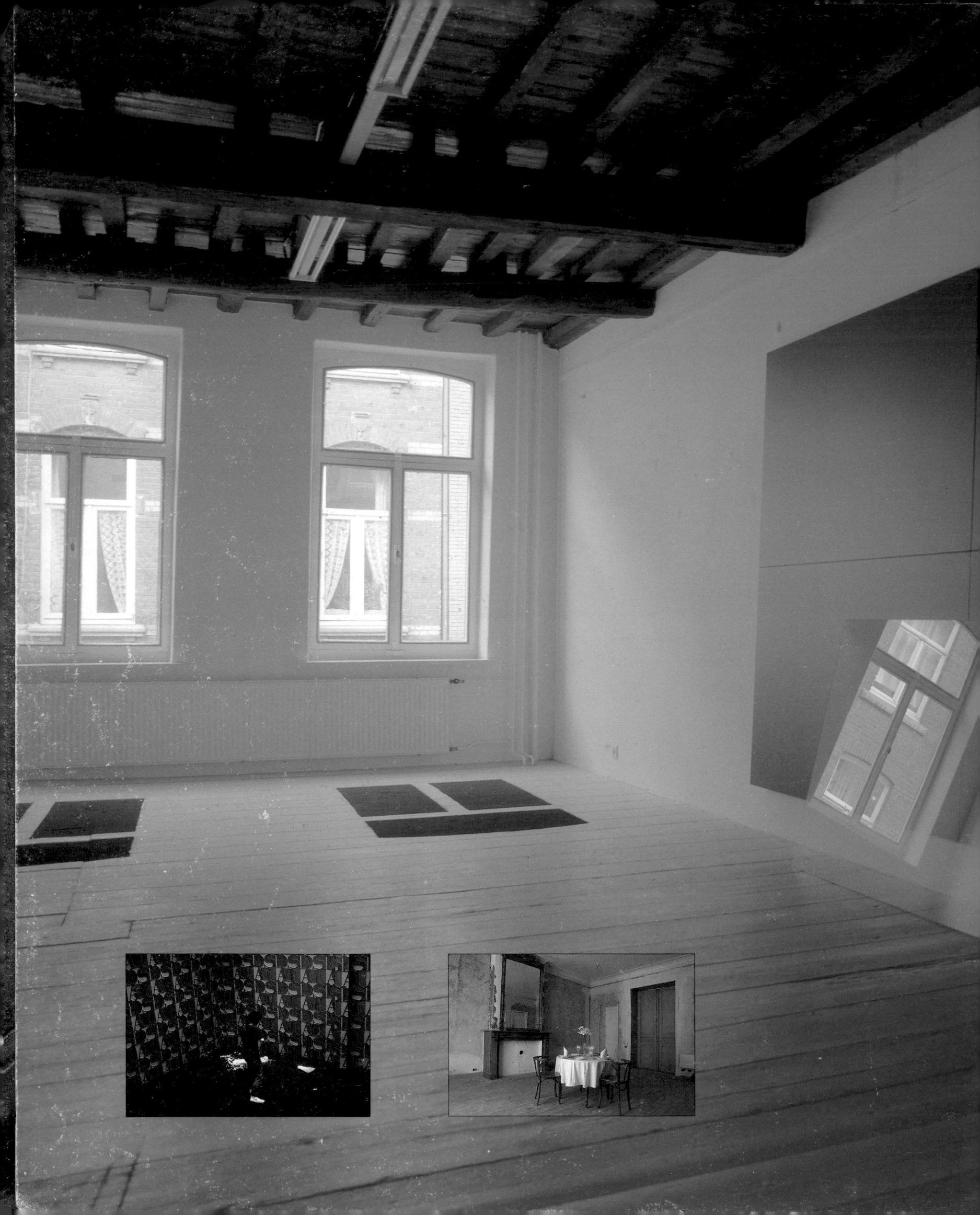

ISSUES/BODY/NARRATIVE

The body as site has become the basis of many installations as in Helen Chadwick's *Blood Hyphen* for the 1988 Edge Biennale, London. Chadwick used a helium neon laser in the upper-half of the Clerkenwell Medical Mission to highlight an enlarged image blowup of cells from her own blood. The image was approached by entering the Church, going down the nave, climbing the pulpit and putting one's head through a removed panel in the horizontally bisected Church. The false ceiling had been installed by the Mission. General Idea's *The AIDS Room from the Pavilion* at the San Francisco Artspace in 1988, featured 27 square inch serigraphed posters papered to the internal walls which read 'AIDS' in the shape of Robert Indiana's 'LOVE' image from the 1960s. Here the physical body is removed into the cultural space and the political battlefield.

Installations though often made as site-specific works, have the ability to project the viewer beyond the boundaries of the given space as they can have strong narrative formats like Kazuo Katase's *Nachtland* (Nightland) at the Gallery Wanda Reiff in Maastricht wherein Katase develops his interest in the philosophical nature of seeing and remembering. The work was bathed in a deep blue light and the large sheets of glass reflected the windows, architecture and photographs that created a narrative space for the viewer to explore. Heike Pallanca's work for the 1986 *Chambre des Amis* exhibition in Belgium featured small inset photographic eyes overseeing the dining room of a house. The rooms used for the exhibition were in the homes of actual residents in Ghent, and Pallanca explored the inherent meaning in the intrusion of the world into our private lives. The viewers' own histories were projected into the personal space through Pallanca's intervention.

MAIN PICTURE: Kazuo Katase, Nachtland, *1990; LEFT: General Idea,* The AIDS Room from the Pavilion, *1988; CENTRE: Heike Pallanca,* Chambre des Amis, *1986; RIGHT: Helen Chadwick,* Blood Hyphen, *1988 (photo: Edward Woodman)*

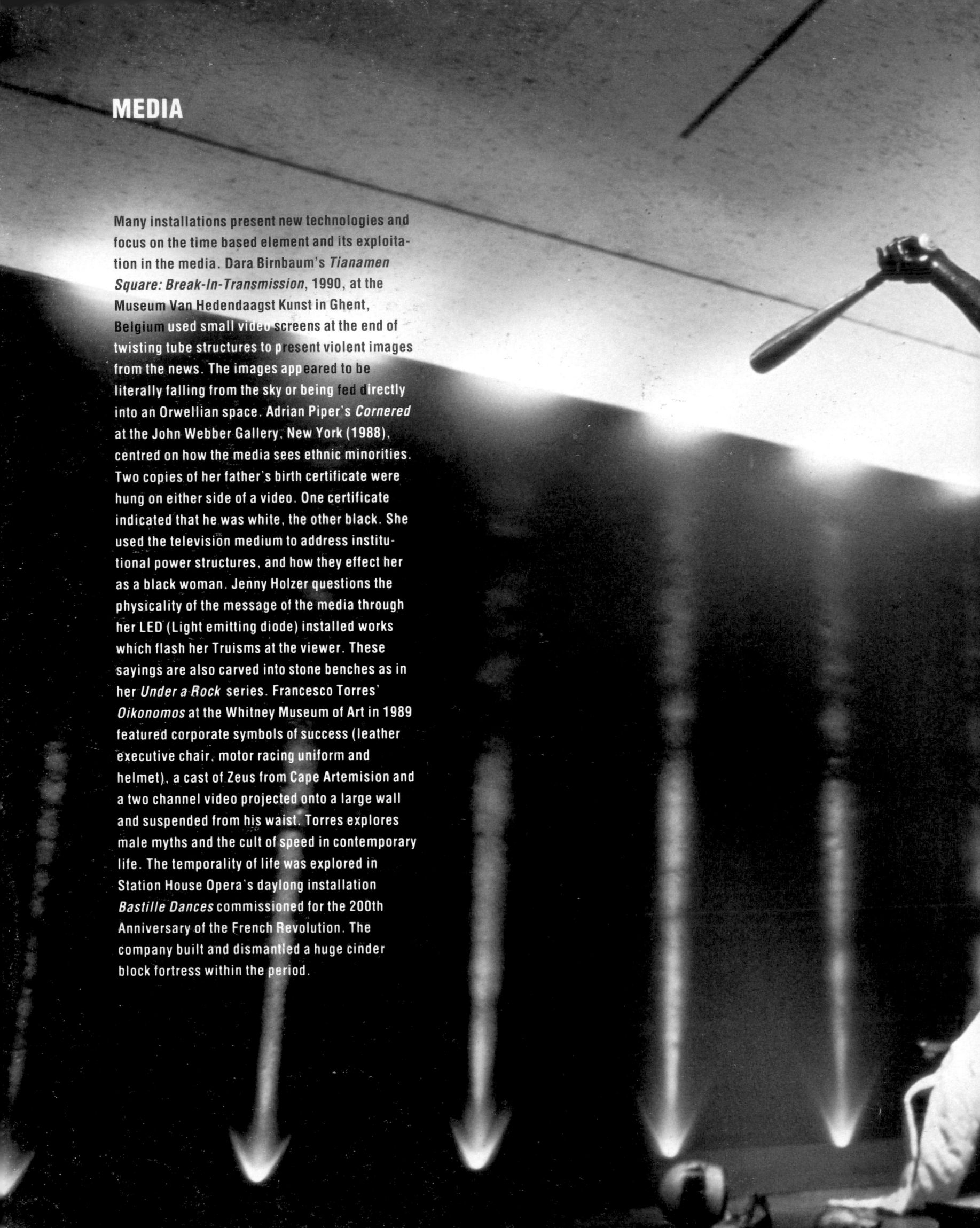

MEDIA

Many installations present new technologies and focus on the time based element and its exploitation in the media. Dara Birnbaum's *Tianamen Square: Break-In-Transmission*, 1990, at the Museum Van Hedendaagst Kunst in Ghent, Belgium used small video screens at the end of twisting tube structures to present violent images from the news. The images appeared to be literally falling from the sky or being fed directly into an Orwellian space. Adrian Piper's *Cornered* at the John Webber Gallery, New York (1988), centred on how the media sees ethnic minorities. Two copies of her father's birth certificate were hung on either side of a video. One certificate indicated that he was white, the other black. She used the television medium to address institutional power structures, and how they effect her as a black woman. Jenny Holzer questions the physicality of the message of the media through her LED (Light emitting diode) installed works which flash her Truisms at the viewer. These sayings are also carved into stone benches as in her *Under a Rock* series. Francesco Torres' *Oikonomos* at the Whitney Museum of Art in 1989 featured corporate symbols of success (leather executive chair, motor racing uniform and helmet), a cast of Zeus from Cape Artemision and a two channel video projected onto a large wall and suspended from his waist. Torres explores male myths and the cult of speed in contemporary life. The temporality of life was explored in Station House Opera's daylong installation *Bastille Dances* commissioned for the 200th Anniversary of the French Revolution. The company built and dismantled a huge cinder block fortress within the period.

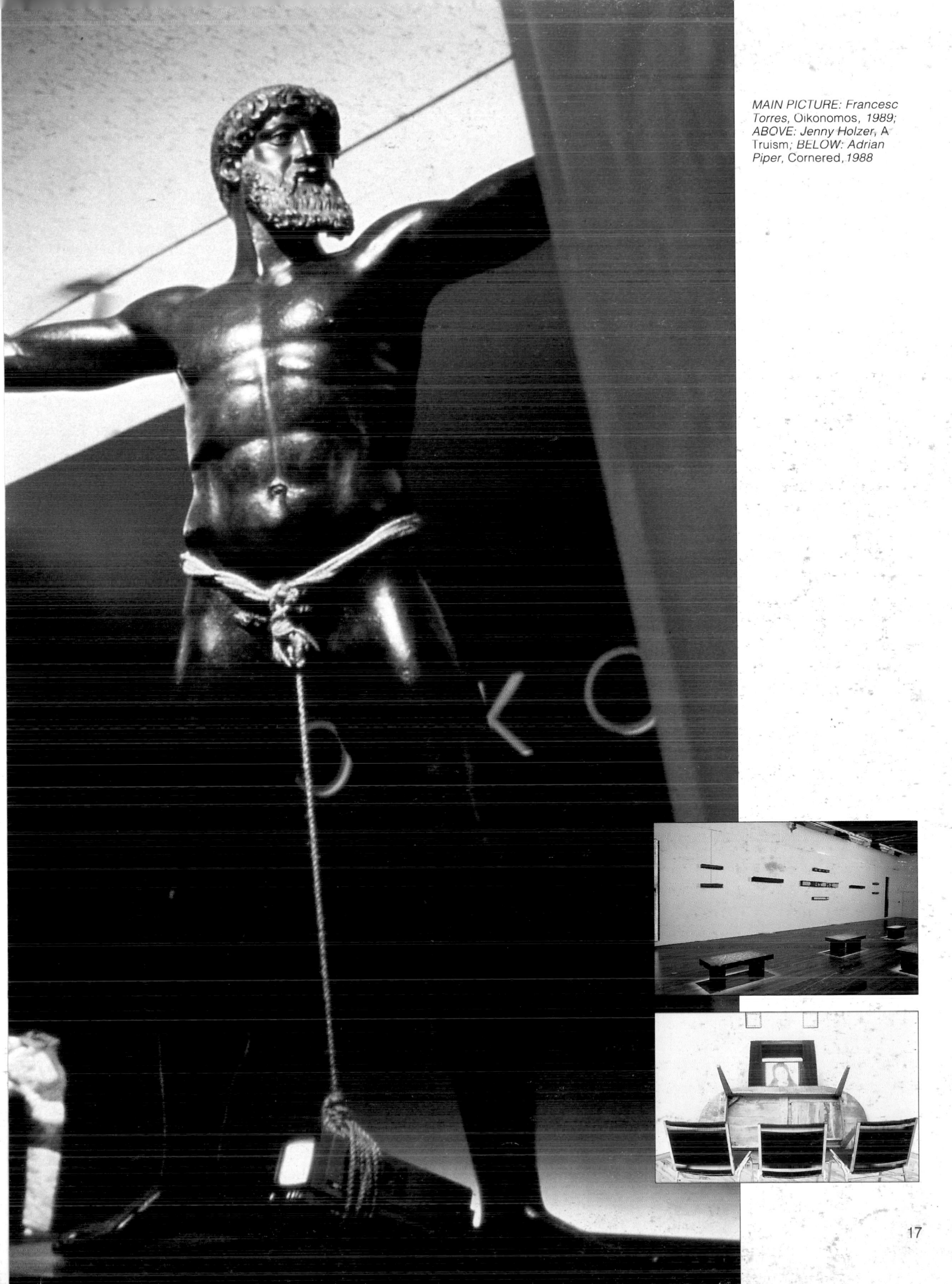

MAIN PICTURE: Francesc Torres, Oikonomos, 1989; ABOVE: Jenny Holzer, A Truism; BELOW: Adrian Piper, Cornered, 1988

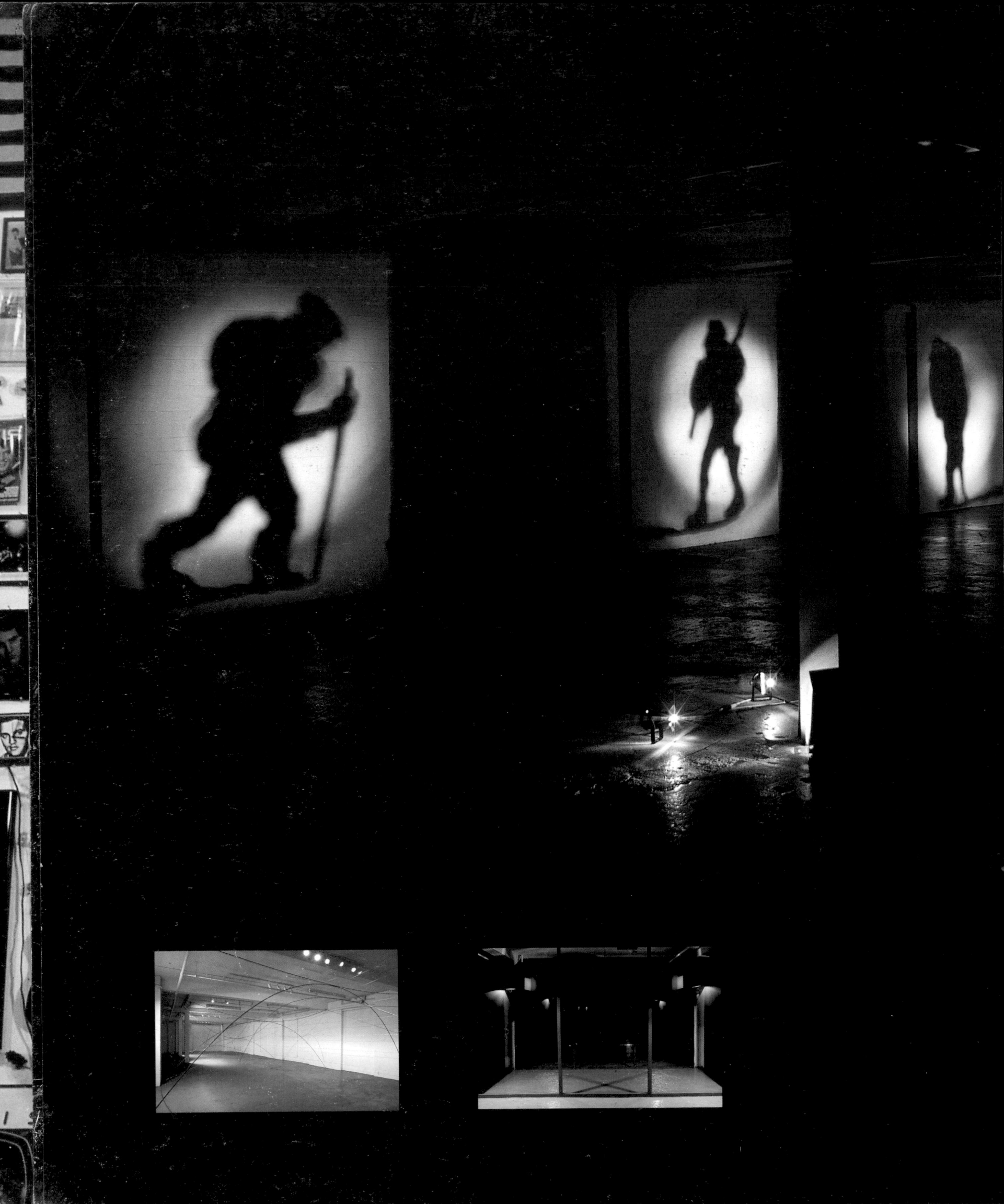

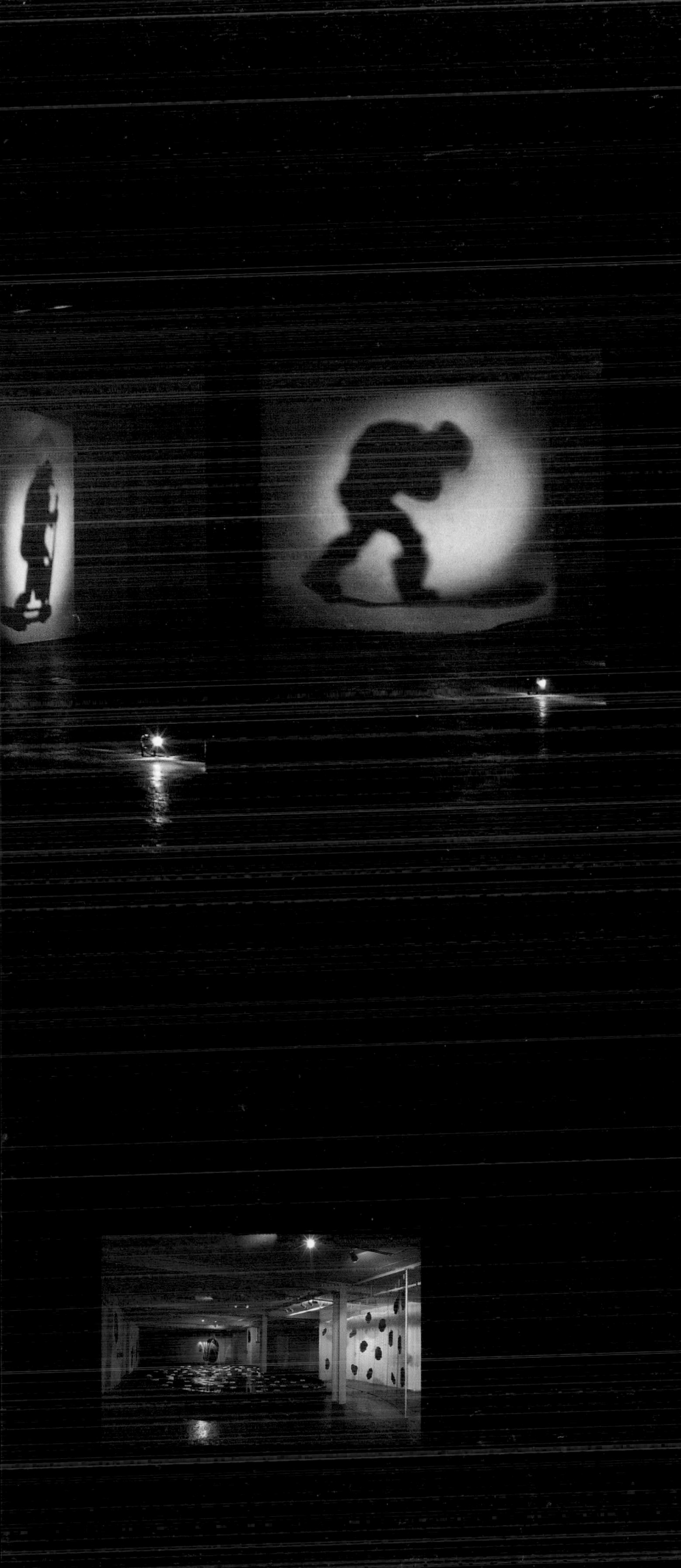

MOI

The following four images are from works at the
Museum of Installation, London from 1991-93.
They depict a range of concerns within installation practice. To be concise the works deal with
many of the issues previously raised, but they
have taken place within the same architectural
container. We believe that this juxtaposition of
images will give the reader a clearer understanding of the breadth of practice within the installation field. Chris Jennings' *Vault* explored the
actual architecture of the site by placing custom
made steel rods in tension in the space. David
Goldenberg investigated the cultural nature of the
site, while Rob Kesseler turned the Museum into
an 'open air' public site in his *Osmosis*, which
featured a large kidney-shaped wading pool and
fountains. Images on the walls were overpainted
with water soluble paint so that the spectators
could wash down the images as in childrens'
colouring books. John Coleman returned the
Museum to its external setting in his *Lapwing,
Redwing, Fieldfare* installation by projecting the
negative image of travellers' silhouettes onto the
gallery's walls. The spectator's own shadow
intermingled with the projected ones as he/she
ambled in the space.

MAIN PICTURE: John Coleman, Lapwing, Redwing,
Fieldfare, 1992; LEFT: Chris Jennings, Vault, 1991;
CENTRE: David Goldenberg, Microwave and Freezer
Stills, Juno 1002; RIGHT: Rob Kesseler, Osmosis

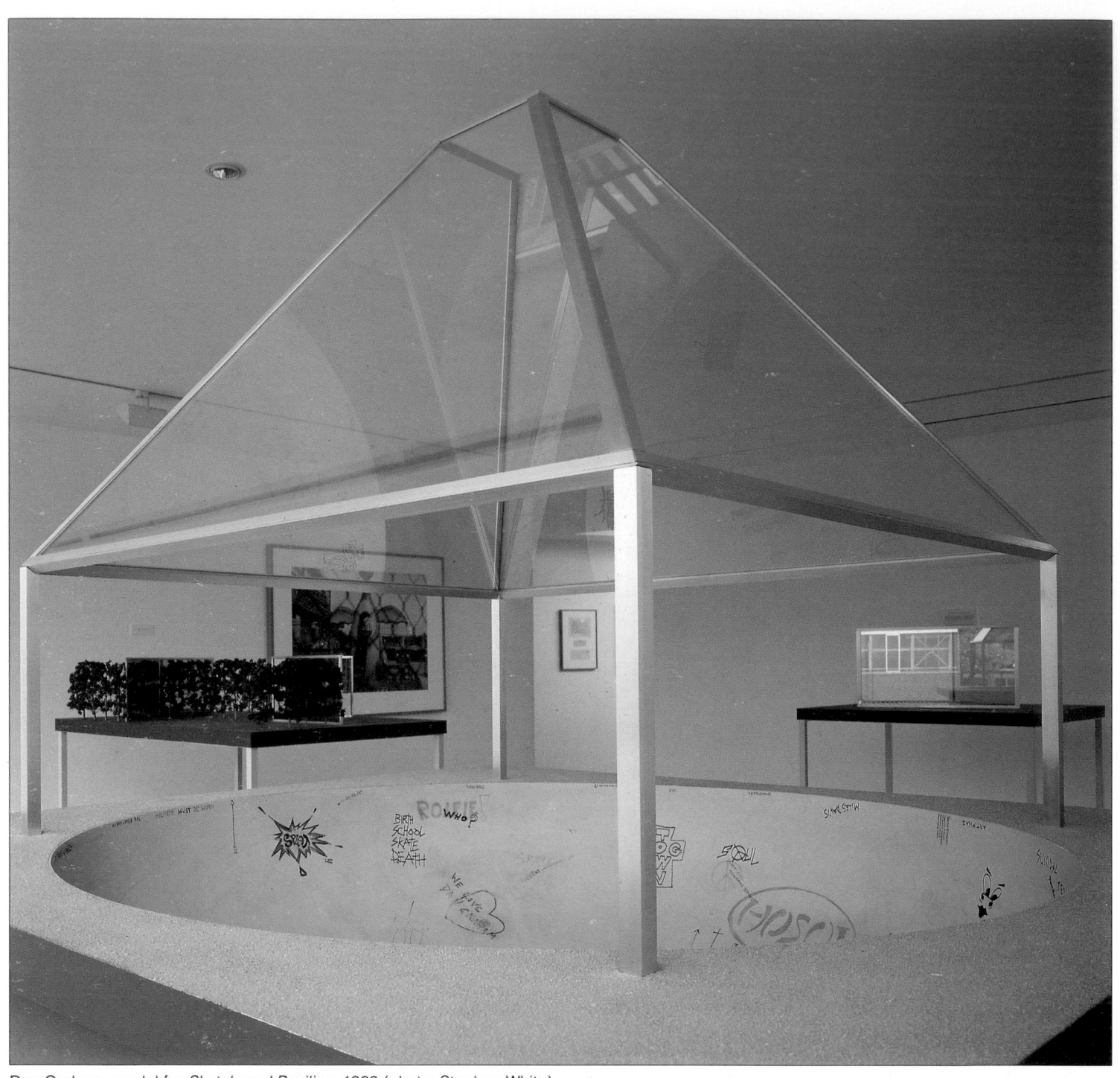

Dan Graham, model for *Skateboard Pavilion*, 1989 (photo: Stephen White)

The Skateboard Pavilion, consisting of a large cement, concave dish for skateboarding and a canopy of two-way mirror glass, a four-sided pyramidal form which is truncated at the top so that it is open, was first proposed for a 'stopping point' for the International Garden Year in 1993 in Stuttgart, Germany. It was not accepted, perhaps because that idea of a recreational attraction primarily for teenagers was not thought to be a good idea. It works maximally when the skateboarder approaches the lip or top edge of the concave dish and looks up towards the sky/canopy and sees a kaleidoscopic reflection and transparency combined image of himself and the surrounding environment on the canopy form. The cut-away top produces a diamond-like image also projected on the two-way mirror canopy. (Dan Graham)

THIERRY DE DUVE
EX SITU

When a site is defined as being the harmony of place, space and scale, it must also be recognised that the history of modern sculpture, hardly heroic, is based on the distressing acknowledgement that there are no more sites.[1] The mountainous amphitheatre at Delphi is a site, the Nevada desert, however, is not; the Capitol at Rome is a site, but the interchange at the entrance of Holland Tunnel is not. It follows, then, that the statues of Apollo and Marcus Aurelius are pieces of art *in situ* and that Michael Heizer's *Double Negative* and Richard Serra's *St John's Rotary Arc* are not; and yet the phrase *in situ* and the theme of art linked to the place in which it exists, were created with regard to these kind of works.

It could be argued that the sculpture of our century, and especially sculpture over the last 20 years, is an attempt to reconstruct the notion of site from the standpoint of having acknowledged its disappearance. So, in that sense, the site of all *in situ* art is a 'non-site', as Robert Smithson once perceptively remarked. With the harmony of place (the cultural tie to ground, territory and identity), space (the cultural consensus on the perceptive grid of reference) and scale (the human body as measure of all things) being doomed to failure, it seems that harmony in a work can only be established between two of these factors, while the third has to be relinquished. Thus, three 'strategies' can be outlined, with each particular one revealing an optimistic moment where the sacrifice of one of the three factors is happily consented to, and a pessimistic moment where, paradoxically, what had been sacrificed finds itself redefined and reinscribed, having acknowledged its failure – a true *in situ* site.

Sacrificing Place, Linking Space and Scale
Is it just by chance that the fourth CIAM (International Congress of Modern Architecture), headed by Le Corbusier which gave rise to the famous Athens Charter, took place on a ship – the *SS Patris* – which had set sail for Marseilles from Athens in the summer of 1933? It was thus on a ship cruising on the Mediterranean that a group of architects proposed a number of cures for the wounds of cities, with the patient in question being the city – a generalised city, for which cures that were just as general were proposed. Man was also generalised, becoming for the CIAM group a sort of abstract citizen defined by *besoins types*[2] and cut up into

functions which were to be distributed into space and 'zones' for living, work, leisure, etc. Not only were the cities of the future planned here but the ideal citizen too; and the only concrete thing that the citizen had to keep was height and bodily proportions. Paragraphs 76 and 87 of the Charter, faithful to a sacred principle in architecture at least since Vitruvius, remind us that all urban dimensions and measurements have to be based on a human scale – a doctrine which, as we know, is at the centre of the idea of the *Modulor* invented by Corbusier. The Athens Charter, which gave its ideological coherence to the International Style, therefore proposed a modernist doctrine which firmly linked space and scale, but at the detriment of place. Everything that tied architecture to local tradition, culture and ground, to a non-universalistic idiom, and to the vernacular, was repressed. It is symbolic that this doctrine was drawn up on a boat and that the liner, Pullman car and aeroplane cabin were, for Corbusier, far more powerful sources of inspiration than anything else created by architecture in the past. His own architecture itself confirms this intention to delocalise. His Villa Savoye, built on pilotis and thus drawn away from the ground as much as possible, is made with materials that completely contrast with the surrounding environment, and are as slightly as possible integrated into the site. It has been noticed that 'Le Corbusier's houses do not age with time and always have to look new'.[3]

It must be noted that behind the sacrifice of place was to be found the idealistic hope of getting rid of private land ownership. Since the causes of damage still exist, it is hardly surprising that the International Style failed, and even less so when you consider that the deterritorialisation of architecture is in the interests of capitalism as espoused by multinational companies. Looking at the worst of the urban realisations we can see just how far its destruction of scale extended. By comparison, Le Corbusier's works suggest a line of resistance of great plastic quality; their essential weakness seems to me to lie instead in a tiny symptom already alluded to: they are not permitted to age.

Another thing that has also aged badly and should be pointed out is all the modern sculpture that tried to intergrate itself with this kind of architecture. To say nothing of the 'biomorphic' or 'Minimal' monsters decorating the esplanades in front of huge office buildings, which look more like giant logos than works of art, it must also be appreciated that great sculptors like Moore and Calder were often compromised into putting their works on sites – or rather non-sites – that made any aesthetic grasp on them impossible. Naum Gabo at the Bijenkorf in Rotterdam is one such failure. However, there had been in Gabo and his brother Antoine Pevsner's doctrine, a strategy reminiscent of Corbusier. According to them, the sculptural object does not make a place materialise by its mass. They oppose a stereometric notion of sculpture against a volumetric one, the former taking sculpture to be an interpenetration of many potential spaces indicated by the object, projecting it in continuity with its surrounding space. Their sculptures often have an empty centre which, rather than bearing witness to the work's presence by its materiality, is a potential source from which the transmutation from place to space occurs.

This shift led them to write, in their *Realistic Manifesto* of 1920, that the space of sculpture did not shape itself from the outside, so that space was defined by solid masses, but from the inside like a unique, coherent and continuous depth, which meant that they naturally favoured transparent materials such as glass, plexiglass and metal wires.[4] Gabo's delocalisation of sculpture is as idealistic as that of Le Corbusier with architecture, and the same optimism and faith in cosmopolitan, universal art, which repudiates any attachment to place can be seen in both artist and architect.[5] It would therefore be worth studying the denial of place by taking into account the work of several artists who, following the manifest failure of the International Style, acknowledged this denial as a loss and made it a condition of comprehending their work. Their vision is disillusioned and pessimistic. Dan Graham's work seems to me to be particularly favourable to such a study, as it lies at the interface of sculpture and architecture, similar to Gabo and Corbusier, but without any illusion of integration. Like Gabo, Dan Graham very often uses transparent and semi-transparent materials with which he constructs what seem to look like architectural objects using the vocabulary of the International Style – *Pavilion/Sculpture for Argonne* for instance. This is a parallelipiped dwelling defined stereometrically, hence its similarity to Gabo, but using a subtle play of partitions of clear glass and semi-clear mirror. It is a sculpture but it is also a pavilion. You therefore enter it and, although you have the feeling that it is exactly at human scale, the kaleidoscopic play of reflections gives you the impression of never knowing exactly where you are. The *here* of the spectator is never a place in the strict sense of the word, it is either a *there* for another spectator watching, or a space reduced by its own reflections. Moreover, the abstraction and the small proportions of the 'object' do not allow for any identification with architecture, and only on careful reflection can a link can be made with a few 'ideal' creations of the International Style – Philip

Johnson's house at New Canaan for one.[6] By contrast, *Alteration to a Suburban House* evokes the real nightmare of modern suburbia. The work is a model of a standardised house similar to the ones reproduced over and over in American suburbs, but the facade has been replaced by a glass screen which reflects the houses opposite and at the same time exposes to the view of the passer-by the petit bourgeois normality of the life taking place inside the rooms giving on to the street. The wall at the far end of the rooms is covered with a mirror which doubles up the spectacle for the inhabitants themselves. The rooms facing the back, however, retain their privacy. It seems to me absolutely essential that such a project, which for now only exists in model form, is never to be constructed, for it basically represents a negative, profoundly pessimistic utopian view, the subject of which is the unfulfilled promise of architectural modernism.[7]

An article by Dan Graham on Gordon Matta-Clark has emphasised the relationship between the two artists' work. In it, Graham underlines the pessimism of Matta-Clark and his refusal to build.[8] Instead of building architectural objects like Graham which divide, fragment and split the place, or planning buildings that are made not to be built, Matta-Clark destroyed or deconstructed existing places and, in one case, literally in two: *Splitting*, realised in Engelwood, New Jersey in 1973, is a suburban house similar to those that Graham targeted in his own work, but older and delapidated, that Matta-Clark split all the way down the middle, cutting through it like an archaeologist excavating the building's past or a surgeon excising a tumour. Parisians are sure to remember Matta-Clark's *Conical Intersect* which he did on a building in the process of demolition, near the Centre Pompidou which was then in construction. The work plays on a complex web of relations with the 'all its insides out' architecture of the Beauborg, as well as with the Eiffel Tower two miles away. It might be worthwhile adding that Matta-Clark only intervened in buildings which were about to be demolished, and the precise cuts that he carried out on them always referred to their particular history.

The optimism of Gabo and Corbusier was thus succeeded by the pessimism of Graham and Matta-Clark, and it is from the acknowlegement of loss of place that these artists associated with site specific art wanted to restore the unity of space and scale. But in doing so, all these concepts were altered and rearticulated. In Graham's case, space and scale are no longer the natural 'givens' or apriorities which form an interdependent harmony, but are completely rethought. It is as if they are quoted for the historic function that they have carried out and the promise they cannot keep. Dan Graham's urban space is no longer the utopian space of the 'Plan Voisin', it is, rather, its deterioration into the American suburb. Consequently, it can no longer be the abstract area of architects' practice, but only a point of reference by the artist playing at being an architect, whose work has critical meaning only if it is made not to be built. It follows that the scale of the model takes on a completely new importance: the model (and Graham insists on this point) must be placed at eye level so the viewer sees it to scale as if he or she lived there. Place is both inexistent – protected onto a future that one hopes is unfeasible – and materialised as a symbolic and institutional place, that of the gallery. Matta-Clark's works, too, end up in a gallery in the form of photographs. But the real place, of which they are the trace, did exist, but does not any longer. Scale, which had been a crucial factor at the time of the physical experience of the work, remains human – not the scale of a Modulor, but of the people who once occupied those places, living there on a day-to-day basis. The urban space Matta-Clark deals with is the space that the anarchy of property development destroys every day – the artist can do little to slow down its ultimate destruction.

Sacrificing Space, Linking Place and Scale

'My purpose is to create a place, not an environment.' This is how Barnett Newman explained his synagogue project begun in 1953; a sacred place – *Makom* in Hebrew – where man, in a state of solitude, can directly experience the transcendence of the Torah. A desire to eliminate the space of painting led Newman from *Onement I* in 1948 to *The Wild* in 1950, a 'shaped canvas' reduced to a 'zip' of 2.4 m in height and 6 cms in width, which allowed him to make the move to his first sculpture, *Here I*, a title suggestive of *Makom*. He has said that the idea for this project came to him while visiting the site of an Indian burial mound in Ohio (which can here be called a site), the force of which was so great that it made the surrounding landscape non-existent.[9] *Here I* is composed of two long upright planks – one narrow plank painted white, and the other wider one covered in plaster – each stuck into a small mound of plaster evoking the Indian mounds. The whole thing, mounted on a whitewashed crate, had been in Newman's studio for at least ten years before he decided to make a bronze mould from it. The crate had probably only been a prop raising the sculpture at the beginning to make the work on it easier, but Newman decided to keep it in. However, when the mould was made the bottle-rack had been left out, so the sculpture rested on the ground, the mounds merging with the surrounding floor space. As this did not turn out to be a satisfactory solution a base in bronze the shape of the crate was made. Bearing the crate in mind, the solution adopted for *Here II* seemed an example of what Newman meant by 'a place' and what I take as being a site abstracted from space or from which one has abstracted the space. *Here II* consists of three vertical planks set into truncated pyramids, themselves sitting on a thick, jagged-edged slab of Cor-ten steel. The way the base has been cut already suggests that it has

been torn away from its own environment, but what highlights this even more is the fact that little casters have been inserted beneath the base out of view, making the sculpture rise by a few centimetres off the ground. To this extent it could be said that what constitutes place for Newman, the *here* of the sculpture, is precisely that which makes it totally independent of every site or every situation. Newman's sculptures are movable and can be put anywhere. They transport their place with them, and with it their sacred power to evoke *Makom*, by flaunting their scorn for the secular space surrounding them. At the same time, they owe their autonomy to the careful gauging of their scale which exceeding human height, glorifies man.

Tony Smith, an architect and a friend of Newman's, moves between Newman's transcendentalism and the 'materialism' of the minimalist generation. His *Six-Foot Cube*, also known as *Die*, from 1962, which is a perfect cube made of black metal, seems to float a few centimetres off the ground, a characteristic it shares with *Here II*. But where the verticality of *Here II*, the varied proportions of the three planks and their placing on the plinth demand that one moves around the sculpture whilst still privileging a frontal view, *Die*, which is identical from every side one looks at it, is unaffected by its positioning. Its geometric ordinariness and black colour accentuate its withdrawal and absorption into itself – it seems deaf to the demands of its surrounding space and blind to the presence of viewers. This absorption, however – to borrow Michael Fried's term – is at the same time the height of theatricality, of which Fried did not fail to accuse him in his famous article 'Art and Objecthood'.[10] Indeed, where *Here II*, by depriving man of the element of *here*, confronted him with his own transcendence, *Die*, by taking the place of man, and excluding him, now only puts him face to face with his own mortality. In Smith's work there lies a tragic spirituality with no redemption in sight and, in place of a rejoicing in humanism, we find a disenchanted insistence on the anthropomorphism of sculpture. The question of scale here is crucial. In exceeding man's height, *Here II* made him taller. *Die* substitutes man as his equal; thus the piece is exactly the same height as man – neither an object nor a monument Smith said – and it also aligns its scale to man. In Smith's work we see a pessimistic version of a strategy which has no trust in social space – the space of exchange which Newman called the environment – in articulating the necessity for something which might have the dignity of a site.

Wherever it might be situated, Smith's *Six-Foot Cube* seems to belong nowhere. It seems completely abandoned, orphaned even, without any reference to anything, as if, rather than it being a sculpture, it were only a plinth. It wasn't the actual statue that was missing so much as the space of communication which makes the statue itself exist and gives it meaning. It is clear that – and this

conditions of *in situ* art in order to better defend the unity of the other two. However, it is not so much the unity that they have safeguarded; but rather the situation of loss that they have negatively redefined and reconstructed. Today, a site is a non-site, and all the alternatives I have given above lead to Robert Smithson, the most lucid theoretician on the subject of site, who reformulated modern negativity into positive terms. Site, as is shown by Graham and Matta-Clark, and interpreted here by Smithson, is the site of urban entropy: 'Has Passaic replaced Rome as the eternal city?'[18] While site, as displayed by Smith and Vermeiren, and again interpreted by Smithson, is that of the museum of emptiness and the emptiness of the museum: 'But I think the nullity implied in the museum is actually one of its major assets, and [that] this should be realised and accentuated.'[19] Finally, site, as shown by Andre and Long and interpreted by Smithson, is that of the traveller making a linear progression through time but taking with him his space-place, endowed, as Smithson says, with 'a double perspective of past and future that follows a projection that vanishes into a non-existant present.'[20]

Notes

1 See R Krauss, 'Echelle/monumentalité, Modernism/ postmodernisme. La ruse de Brancusi', in *Qu'est-ce que la sculpture moderne?*, Centre Georges Pompidou, Paris, 1986, p246.

2 'Besoins types, meubles types' is the title of a chapter in Le Corbusier's *L'art décoratif d'aujourd' hui* (first published 1925), Vincent Fréal, Paris, 1959.

3 J-M Richards, *L'architecture moderne*, Paris, Poche, 1968, p212.

4 See Margit Rowell, 'Constructivisme', in *Qu'est-ce que la sculpture moderne?, op cit*, p66.

5 See her *Passages in Modern Sculpture,* Viking, New York, 1977, pp56-61

6 Built in 1949, Johnson's Glass House is a radical realisation of one idea of transparency in modernist architecture. It is ideal in the sense that the architect built it for himself and thus was not to compromise in any way. It is situated in a large private park so Johnson doesn't have to worry about passers-by and neighbours looking in. *Pavilion/Sculpture for Argonne* is also situated in a private park; it belongs to the Argonne National Laboratory who commissioned the piece, but kept it open to the public.

7 The project was made in 1978 and is akin to *Homes for America*, one of Dan Graham's first pieces, published in *Arts Magazine*, December 1966.

8 Dan Graham, 'Gordon Matta Clark' in *Flyktpunkter/ Vanishing Points*, catalogue, Moderna Museet, Stockholm, 1984.

9 cf Thomas Hess, *Barnett Newman*, New York, MOMA, 1971, p73.

10 Michael Fried, 'Art and Objecthood', *Artforum*, June 1969, republished in Gregory Battcock ed, *Minimal Art*, Dutton, New York, 1968; see also Fried's *Absorption and Theatricality, Painting and the Beholder in the Age of Diderot*, University of California Press, Berkeley, 1980.

11 See R Krauss' article 'Echelle/monumentalité', *op cit* p247 and Benjamin HD Buchloch, 'Construire (l'histoire de) la sculpture' in *Qu'est-ce que la sculpture moderne?, op cit*, p254.

12 See Thierry de Duve, 'Didier Vermeiren', *+ - 0*, no 15, 1976, and L'ancien avenir' in *Tournai*, catalogue, Tournai, 1979.

13 See Michael Assenmaker's excellent article 'De la photographie à la sculpture chez Didier Vermeiren: éléments de lecture', in *Didier Vermeiren* catalogue, Palais des Beaux-Arts, Brussels, 1987.

14 See Marielle Tabart, 'Introduction', in *Brancusi photographe*, Centre Georges Pompidou, Paris, 1979, p10.

15 Quotations are from *Carl Andre: Sculpture 1959-1977*, text by David Bourdon, Jaap Rietman Inc, New York, 1978, p27.

16 Quoted by Lucy Lippard, *Six Years: The Dematerialisation of the Art Object*, Praeger, New York, 1973, p47.

17 M Fried, 'Art and Objecthood', *op cit*, p134.

18 Nancy Holt ed, *The Writings of Robert Smithson*, New York University Press, New York, 1979, p56.

19 *ibid*, p60.

20 *ibid*, p211.

ANDREW BENJAMIN
MATTER AND MEANING: ON INSTALLATIONS

Taking up the installation involves locating it within the continual attempt to ground the specificity of art. A consequence of this location involves accepting the premise that the installation's meaning is, in part, structured by its own negotiation with the question of art. With such a negotiation, art is present as a question.

As will be indicated, installation's work – its effective presence – is sanctioned by the question remaining open. The installation is at work within that opening.

A start can be made therefore by working with the already present recognition that one of the questions around which art continues to turn concerns what it is that gives the work its specific quality as art. In other words what is it that allows a given material object to exist as a work of art? It goes without saying that the art market, fashion and the continual slide from art work to commodity form an integral part of any answer to such a question. And yet there remains something unsatisfactory about their inclusion in any answer if, as a consequence, it is thought to be complete.

In general terms art has, of course, continually addressed, and had addressed for it, the question of what it is. Moreover the specific forms within art – painting, sculpture, etc – have been subject to the same attempt to secure and establish their own boundaries. The attempt within the Kantian and therefore modernist tradition to differentiate 'fine art', or more simply the 'beautiful' from mere representation, even from a mimetic presentation of 'fine art' or the 'beautiful', was the attempt to establish that which was unique about the work of art. Not only painting but sculpture and the other 'fine arts' were included in the attempt to maintain a justified differentiation of art from non-art. It should not be thought, however, that this distinction remains secure. Indeed it is possible to argue that it has become increasingly less stable. (Working with the slip of stability helps mark out in the contemporary in art practices.)

Instability should not be too rapidly generalised since it is usually established either as the consequence of a specific interpretation or by the advent of new art practices. In the case of the former what this means is that the distinction, art/non-art, comes undone by showing – showing as interpreting – the fragility and in the end the impossibility of maintaining the distinction as absolute and thus as all inclusive. In the latter it is that the advent of film and more recently video, for example, has had the effect of mediating, and in the end frustrating, any attempt to secure the distinction. Both of these presentations are such that their very nature makes it difficult to incorporate them in a straightforward and unproblematic way on either side of the art/non-art divide. As a result therefore, that which holds the division up is brought into question.

There is, however, another possibility. Another reason why the distinction between art and its other will always be marked by a potential instability. As a beginning the reason is art's materiality. Its material and physical presence announces that despite everything else the work of art is an object, a material object. Nonetheless in taking up the work of art, its materiality is often effaced in favour of the consequence of art's material presence. Emphasising, for example, the way in which the work of sculpture creates space, necessitates the absorption of the materiality such that the materiality is repositioned as the support of spacing. Materiality works by its buttressing of the object's art work. If, in contradistinction to the effacing of material presence, it is made central, then the question of what counts as a work immediately opens up. This repositioning of matter and therefore, of the materiality of the art object is not to be taken as a simple empiricism. Matter on its own however, is not sufficient. Matter is not an end in itself. With matter, what will also have to be introduced is the impossibility of positing materiality as present – as having a specific presence – outside of the operation of signification. Matter is given with meaning.

One way of taking the interplay of matter, meaning and the objectivity of art leads inexorably to the problem of ornamentation, another way leads to a specific type of questioning that finds its most insistent source in Duchamp and therefore with the ready-made and the installation assumes, none the less, that the latter derives, in part, its condition of existence from the former.

It is not necessary here to rehearse the complex impact of the ready-made. All that needs to be indicated is that with it the problem of objectivity and thus what is to count as a work of art is intensified. An object that already existed and hence which was already located outside the sphere of art – the sphere minimally constructed by the interrelated presence of exhibition and criticism/interpretation – was incorporated into that sphere by it being exhibited and thus located within the margins of art practice. The problem to be faced is accounting for how it is that what was initially excluded has come to be included. Starting by working from the other direction what can be asked for, at least initially, is an account of both how the exclusion could have been maintained, and then why it should have been maintained in the first place.

Now, it is tempting to argue that a given object should not have been included because of the precise nature of its materiality. However, that is on its own far from adequate since what must be added is that an essential part of its non-inclusion would be that it was already located within a defined set of established meanings. In other words, that integral to any argument for its not being art is that its meaning was already established. It had a meaning which, by definition would have to be argued, fell outside of the purview of art. Materiality therefore, as has been suggested, is already positioned within an already present structure of meaning. Recognising this ineliminable reciprocity between meaning and matter overcomes the threat of empiricism.

With this present positioning there are three different points which, in being made, allow for the inherent complexity of this set up to be indicated. These three points sanction certain strategic interconnections. Tracing these relationships will occasion the place of the installation to be opened up. The first point is that while the material presence of art – the frame and the canvas, for example – works to locate the painting within the sphere of art, the work of that material presence also precludes its absorption into another domain of meaning. What this entails here is that it is painting's materiality which works to hold it in place. The second point is that what makes the ready-made important is that it indicates that this restriction does not work, in any straightforward way, when the reverse situation pertains. In other words that ready-made is to be admitted to the domain of art, initially at least, simply in virtue of its materiality. What emerges retrospectively is that its material presence is neither completely held nor absolutely determined by the structure of meaning in which it is articulated. There is an important distinction to be drawn here therefore, between types of determination; ie the determination of matter within the sphere of art as opposed to the determination outside it.

The materiality of the object overcomes its location and meaning outside of the sphere of art. In part this is because matter while always presented in terms of function, does not lose its materiality once the given function no longer pertains. It is thus that the ready-made could be taken as being the supreme articulation of art as without purpose. This may well be the limit of the ready-made. Indeed it is possible to go further and argue that while the ready-made opened up the possibility of the installation by opening up the question of the art object – it occupied an ambivalent position. The ambivalence emerges because it involves both a simple reiteration, albeit in another form, of the classical determination of 'purposiveness without a purpose', while at the same time sustaining its own irreducibility to function while presenting, even if in a non-functional form, that which has (or had) a function. This ambivalence creates an opening that is founded in matter and it will be the opening of matter and with it the opening of the art object that will work to locate the site of installation.

The final point that arises here, which can also be linked to the above, concerns sculpture. Once matter is taken into consideration then the relation between art and non-art will be at its most complex in relation to sculpture. Part of the complexity involves the relationship that material presence has both to ornament and to function. A constituent element of sculpture's role was to ornamentalise. In being an ornament, its function was reduced to its being-as-ornament. Sculpture as either monument or symbol was defined by its specific being. This definitional hold on sculpture, however, is freed with abstraction; the process of abstraction. And yet the freedom in question is delimited by function. It is checked by it and consequently its work is held by the relationship between matter and function; the latter will always allow for its own negative presence.

What this means is that to the extent that abstraction held itself apart from function, what was presented was assumed to be the simple materiality of the sculptural, its form. With abstraction therefore, sculpture is taken up with the possibility of it being the enactment of the purity and simplicity of form. Without here attempting to investigate the viability of this possibility what must be noted is that the freedom of abstraction, the process of abstracting – albeit what in the end is an illusory freedom – in enacting the arbitrary hold of function and ornament, opens up as a question that which will, henceforth, control and delimit material presence.

With sculpture the arbitrary will be introduced. What it is that will count as sculpture will incorporate the arbitrary for two reasons. The first is that the arbitrary stems from the indeterminancy of signification resulting from the break up of the tight relation between sculpture, function and ornament. Secondly, it arises because of sculpture's materiality. It is clear that these reasons are connected. The result is that the materiality of sculpture will allow, potentially, for any material form to be presented as sculpture. Matter's presence is no longer fixed by its primary site of signification. Of the many possibilities this founding lack of fixity will allow, one of the most insistent, will be the installation. Installations, however, through the nature and divergence of their work will no longer be held by the problems posed by materiality. They will work with them in opening up other adventures and activities.

The departure that sets up and identifies the practice of the installation will also be linked to the ready-made. With the ready-made what occurs is that the interruption of the signifying system in which the object was initially located disrupts the space in which it comes to be placed. Originally the material presence of the object entails that its meaning was never such that the matter and meaning were co-extensive even if they were delimited by function. (Again it is an original plurality that only emerges retrospectively.) The relocation of the object, its transformation into a work of art, derives its conditions of existence for that founding lack of co-extensivity – a lack stemming from matter and which will always be in excess of simple functionality – and then reproduces the impossibility of that closure in its transformation into an object. The ready-made carries its original function but always opens itself beyond it, and in not being reducible, it allows for, by incorporating, a spacing. It is this spacing that was originally given with the first relation between matter and meaning and which gets reinscribed in

(and into) the object's transformation. In the latter case the spacing allows matter to do art's work. It will be a work, however, that in falling beyond the hold of symbol, ornament and function eschews, at the same time, the hold of prediction. The work in question will incorporate the art of installation.

What allows, initially, installations to have their effect is their position both to sculpture and the ready-made. It is a relation that is itself only made possible and thus given the space to work – thus also for work – because of matter and matter's relation to meaning. Art's material presence, present here with the installation, founds and confounds sites of signification and in so doing allows for a practice that in the continuity of the creation of a topos and thereby in the resisting of restrictions, continues an opening of meaning. This continuity is the work of art

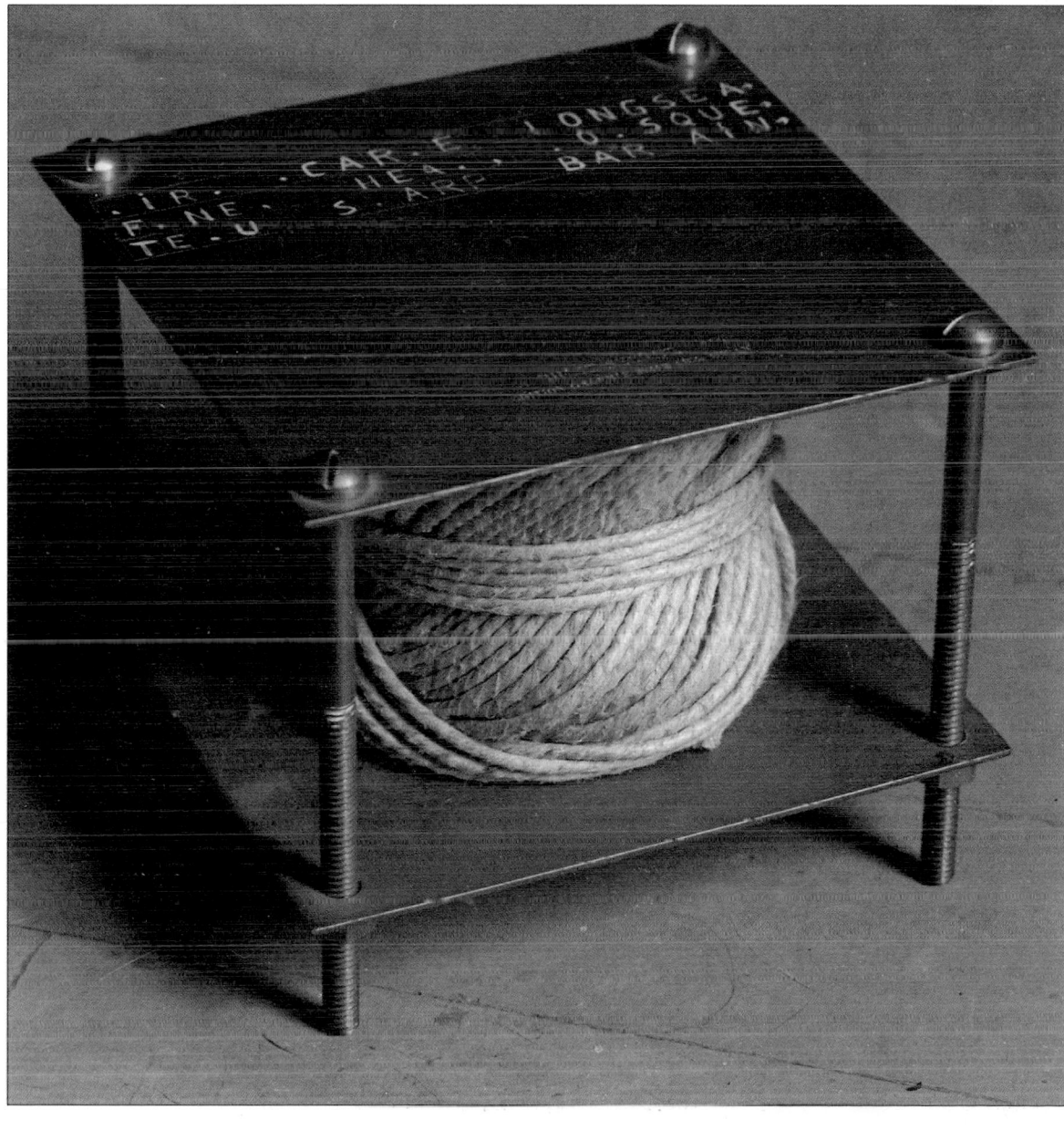

Marcel Duchamp, With Hidden Noise, *1916*

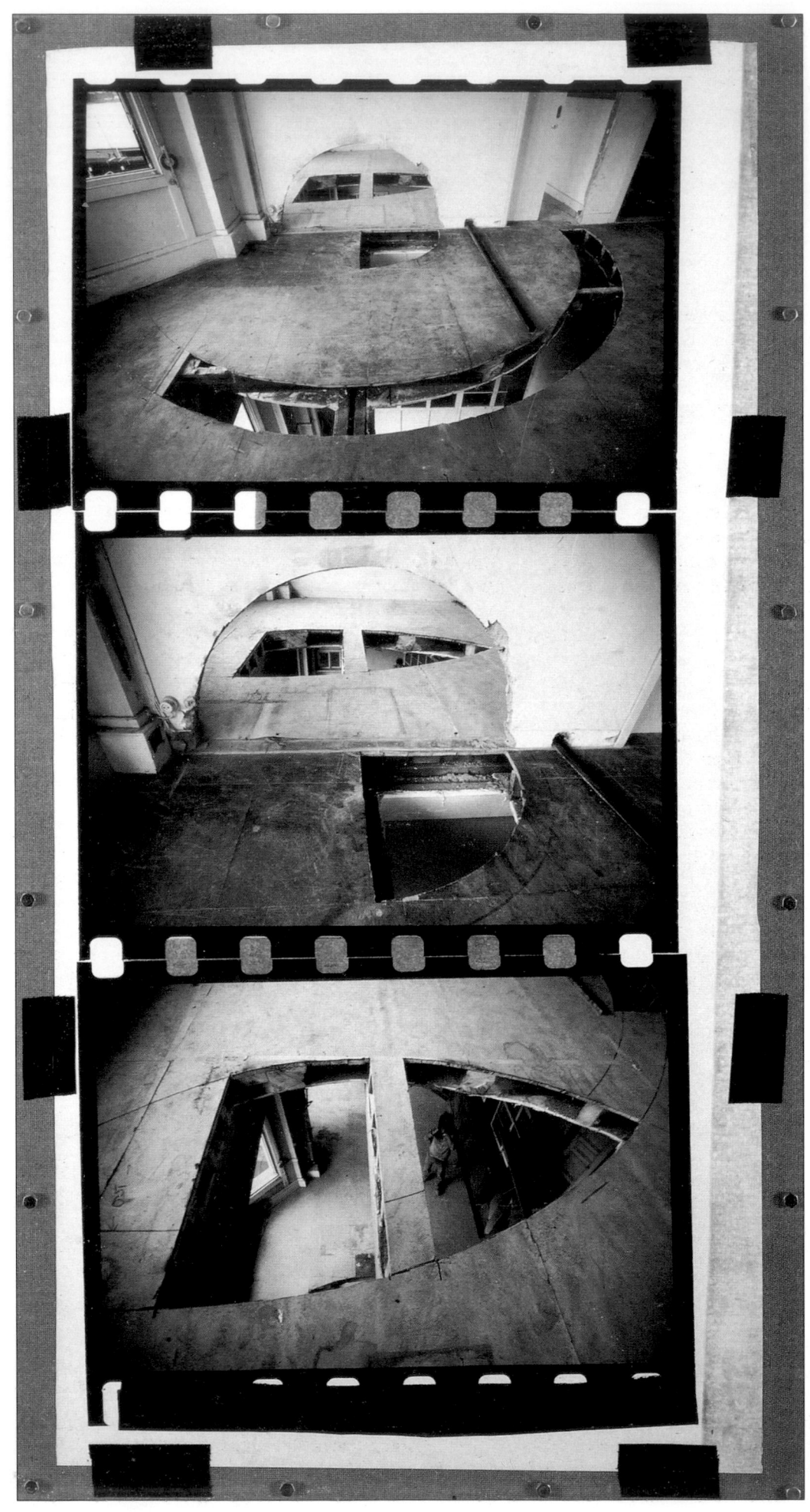

CORINNE DISERENS
GORDON MATTA-CLARK

The late 60s and early 70s was a time of conflict and questioning in American society. Avant-garde young artists started to group themselves in the warehouses and factories of Soho. They were characterised by a shared interest in experimentation, immediacy and urgency – the process of making work being the primary concern. There was a real desire to extend the definition of what was considered art and to alter the established structure of the art world. Increasingly these artists felt it necessary to take control of their own context by creating alternative spaces and charting new territories beyond the object and beyond the gallery.

The official American discourse in art was almost exclusively dominated by the Greenbergian canon. The Post-Minimalist conviction that painting had come to an end must be seen against this background. They were directly opposed to Clement Greenberg's principle of honesty in art, choosing instead to reveal the real world behind the sacred surface. It is interesting that Matta-Clark implicitly referred to Lucio Fontana when he described the act of opening up illusory art space in order to work 'upon the real world'. 'I don't think they (io Achor and Druce Nauman) ever penetrated the surface, which would seem the next logical step'.[1]

> When architects pretend to produce spatial architecture, they remain on the ground and this is an enormous mistake because they only introduce elements in space, they never make a spatial structure. (Fontana).

Matta-Clark was a pivotal figure in the Soho community. Son of Anne Clark and the Chilean painter Roberto Matta, he studied architecture at the Cornell School of Architecture (1962-68). His relationship to architecture was conflicting and complex.[2] In 1976 he was invited to participate in the exhibition 'Idea as Model', organised by the Institute of Architecture and Urban Studies in New York, and curated by the architect Andrew MacNair. At that time Peter Eisenman was the Institute's director. The show included projects by various architects such as Michael Graves and Richard Meier. Matta-Clark's first proposal was to cut one of the closed, airless seminar rooms into two-by-two-foot-square pieces. Instead of making this formal work in a gallery space an inoffensive commentary, Matta-Clark made a work that quite literally took aim at the Institute itself. He borrowed Dennis Oppenheim's gun and he came to the gallery at 3 am. After he had blown out the windows of the exhibition hall, he lined each

window casement with a photograph of a new housing project in the South Bronx, whose windows had been smashed by the residents. That same night, before the exhibition opening, the windows were replaced, and 'the piece was eliminated' (MacNair).

Suddenly a situation 'external' to architecture – the 'otherness' of the South Bronx, which could be subjected to theories of health and sanitation – had changed to an intimate situation 'internal' to architecture. For one brief moment the Institute itself had been turned into a South Bronx building, subjected to the threat of violence. Matta-Clark's provocative act confronts those secret fears that won't be sublimated into the dialectics of interior and exterior: 'Glass symbolism is incorporated in every smashed window'[3, 4]

Gordon Matta-Clark used houses and building structures which were abandoned or about to be demolished, and revealed 'hidden layers of socially concealed architectural and anthropological family meaning'. His work functions as a kind of urban 'agit-prop', something like the acts of the Paris Situationalists in 1968, who had seen their acts as public intrusions or 'cuts' in the seamless urban fabric.[5] Matta-Clark was 'discreetly violating' the cycle of endless architectural consumption, and his building cuts were exposing the containerisation of usable space in the interests of capitalism.

> By undoing a building . . . [I] open a state of enclosure which had been preconditioned not only by physical necessity but by the industry that proliferates suburban and urban boxes as a pretext for ensuring a passive, isolated consumer.[6]

Matta-Clark had reflected on similar ideas in earlier works such as *Open House*,1972. But ultimately the determining factor for him was the degree to which his intervention could transform the structure into an act of communication. What interested him in breaking through the surface, was the thin edge of what was being seen, as much as the views that were created. He aimed to reveal how a uniform surface was established – the layering, the different things that were being served – how the simplest solution was to create complexity. But he literally inscribed himself within the building. Precisely in this physical act, transgression was contained – digging up foundations, cutting through ceilings, walls and floors in often dangerous situations that required a precarious balance. The insides were like

OPPOSITE: Office Baroque, *1977*

112 Greene Street, 1971

During 1971, Gordon Matta-Clark created a series of installations *in situ* in the basement of the legendary space opened by Jeffrey Lew at 112 Greene Street. The first, *Cherry Tree*, was started on the morning of New Year's Day. 'I dug a deep hole in the basement of 112 Green Street. What I wanted to do I didn't accomplish at all, which was digging deep enough so that a person could see the actual foundations, the "removed" spaces under the foundation, and liberate the building's enormous compressive, confining forces simply by making a hole. To be able to pass freely under an area once so dominated by gravitational constraint – that would have been something!

Another installation I had for Greene Street, which I was a bit reluctant about since it might have jeopardised the people in the building was to have cut each column at midpoint and insert a small steel cube. Where digging a hole liberated compression, this one would have done the opposite: concentrated the entire building's forces onto those little cubes. The cubes then would have balanced the building: an identity transference. The sheer compressive energy being invoked would have made, I think, the physical reality of confronting those cubes a fairly threatening experience.'[1]

This project was not carried out, and instead Matta-Clark planted a tree in the hole in the basement. In the pile of earth left over he planted grass seed and over the whole installation he hung infrared lights. This work survived for three months, while the tree remained alive. During this period Matta-Clark devoted himself to looking for rubbish, waste materials and abandoned spaces with a view to reclaiming them. The artist spent some time collecting old bottles with the aid of various friends, including Jeffrey Lew. In the winter of 1971, part of the material was used to create *Winter Garden: Mushroom and Waistbottle Recycloning Cellar*, also known as *Glass Plant*. The bottles were piled up in an old street elevator under the steps to the basement of 112 Greene Street, where he also installed a glass furnace. In the place where *Cherry Tree* had been previously he planted mushrooms. With the furnace he melted the glass and made what he called 'commemorative ingots'. One day, accidentally, the furnace was left on all night and all the bottles melted except one, in which he put cherry fruit and stones from *Cherry Tree*.

In June of the same year, in the hole dug for the tree, Matta-Clark created another work: *Time Well*. 'Working with the facts and fabric of building space *Time Well* is a permanent non-structural sub-basement burial. Using architectural components to extend a room beyond its common limits, through a play of functional connections, the piece substitutes an implied perspective for frontality. An 8'x4'x6' hole was excavated for an earlier work. In refilling it a watertight ceramic shaft 6 feet deep and 10 inches square was set in a concrete footing and buried. Over the earth fill a slab was poured to match the concrete basement floor. Lead-filled lines in the concrete mark the area of the original cavity – the remaining *Time Well* contains a fermenting preparation of cherry fruit and pits.'[2]

A W-hole House: Roof Top Atrium and Datum Cut, 1973

'The *Datum Cuts*, for example took place in an engineers' drafting rooms and offices. I couldn't deal with the outside because there wasn't enough exterior enclosure to really penetrate anything. What fascinated me was the interior central plan. The engineers took a small, square, primitive hut shape and divided it in half to make one big drafting room. They divided the other half into a quarter which became the office, and divided the remaining quarter in half again for the coatroom and bathroom. Everything was progressively divided so that the remaining last piece was 1/32 of the whole. I used the idea of decision around the centre. Therefore, I removed a square section out of the roof apex (*Roof Top Atrium*), then projected that cut from the roof down into the building and spread it out laterally through the walls and doors (*Datum Cut*). The walls in Italy are fascinating because they hold a good fine chisel line without falling apart [. . .] The act of cutting through from one space to another produces a certain complexity involving depth perception. Aspects of stratification probably interest me more than the unexpected views which are generated by the removals – not the surface, but the thin edge, the severed surface that reveals the autobiographical process of its making. There is a kind of complexity which comes from taking an otherwise completely normal, conventional, albeit anonymous situation and redefining it, retranslating it into overlapping and multiple readings of conditions past and present. Each building generates its own situation.'[3]

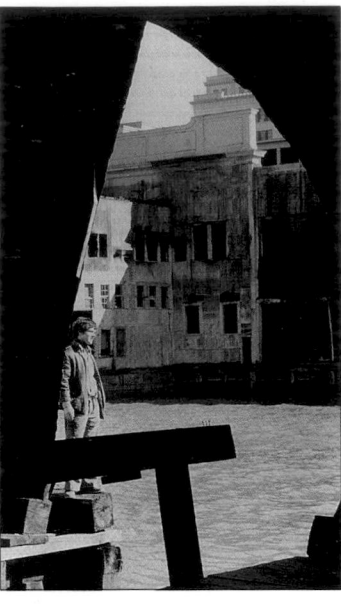

A W-hole House was the title of the exhibition which was subsequently held in Galleriaforma with sections of the wall and the roof of the building and photographic pieces of the work. Other photographs, drawings and cut stacks of paper which were connected with the project *Infraform* were also presented, together with other works produced in New York.

Splitting, 1974

'*Splitting* was done at 332 Humphrey Street in Engelwood, New Jersey. It was a predominantly Black neighbourhood that was being demolished for an urban renewal project that was never completed. When I took over the house, it was strewn with personal debris left by its abruptly evicted tenants. The work began by cutting a one-inch slice through all the structural surfaces dividing the building in half. The second stage was to bevel down the 40 lineal feet of the foundation so that the rear half could be lowered one foot. The central "split" was formed by the five degree tilt activating the house with a brilliant wedge of sunlight that spilled into every room.'[4]

The artist made further alterations on the second floor which affected the four side corners. Where the ceiling and the outside walls came together in each corner, a six-sided cut with six right angles was made. On one side of the house the separated pieces were left in place; on the other they were removed at the front and the rear.

On the day of the opening, in June, Holly Solomon hired a bus to make it easier to get to Engelwood. The inaccessibility and unstable appearance of the house and the risk involved in walking in the cut structures turned the visit into a kind of performance. Alice Aycock recalls: 'Starting at the bottom of the stairs where the crack was small, you'd go up, and as you'd go further up you'd have to keep crossing the crack. It kept widening as you made your way up the stairs to the top, the crack was one or two feet wide. You really had to jump it. You sensed the abyss in a kinesthetic and psychological way.'[5] Horace Solomon's account also communicates this unease: 'After it had been cut I felt nervous being in the house, I thought it would collapse any minute. I really didn't enjoy being in it, though I loved the way it looked from outside, and liked standing back and looking at it.'[6]

Splitting provoked highly irate reactions from other architects. 'One of them sent me a letter accusing me of violating the sanctity and dignity of abandoned buildings by interrupting their natural transition to decay or demolition. Another person saw what I did as out-and-out rape. There were also occasional accusations (particularly because of my architectural training) of my occupying an ideological position diametrically opposed to the practising architect and to all that the profession implicates regarding human problems.'[7]

ABOVE: Gordon Matta-Clark

Day's End, 1975

'To a small degree *Day's Passing*, done at Pier 52 in New York City in 1975, was a step in the right direction. I didn't have any illusion about the causes, only about making a mark in a sad moment of history. This piece is on the Hudson River and is the only one of my works to have survived over two years. As it stands in New York's most dramatically neglected historical area, this pier has turned into a mugger's lane for the sexual underground community. Technically, under the jurisdiction of the City Port Authority, their level of disinterested abandonment virtually removed the property from the realm of society. I simply took it over until the project was finished. Pier 52 is an intact 19th-century industrial relic of steel and corrugated tin looking like an enormous Christian basilica whose dim interior was barely lit by the clerestory windows 50 feet overhead.

The initial cuts were made through the pier floor across the centre forming a tidal channel nine feet wide by 70 feet long. A sail-shaped opening provides access to the river. A similar shape through the roof directly above this channel allows a patch of light to enter which arches over the floor until it's captured at noon within the watery slot. During the afternoon the sun shines through a cat-eye-like 'rose window' in the west wall. At first a sliver and then a strongly defined shape of light continues to wander into the wharf until the whole pier is fully illuminated at dusk. Below the rear 'wall-hole' is another large quarter-circular cut opening the floor of the south-west corner to a turbulent view of the Hudson water. The water and sun move constantly in the pier throughout the day in what I see as an indoor park, a-sun-and-water-temple.'[8]

Office Baroque, 1977

'Antwerp has fulfilled my artistic needs for a conservative and resistant encounter, at least on an official level. Personally, I had a wonderful ally in Flor Bex at the ICC and a wonderful result. The original idea for this piece was based on the fact that the building is in one of the most conspicuous areas of town – right in front of the Steen, the quintessence of a touristic hot spot where everyone comes to snap a shot. This work, like the majority of my other works, was conceived of as an exterior of the building, something that would have had a spherical quadrant removed from the corner of the building allowing sightseers to see through it. Once the city found out what was planned, they killed the project. Luckily the owner, the MP-Omega NV allowed me to continue only if I promised to work completely out of public view inside the building. This gave me the enforced opportunity to develop ideas about spatial rhythm and complexity that I might have otherwise never done. In making this shift from a public to private work, the formal decisions passed through a curious sequence. My first five-storey building had unique potentials and I wanted to work out an almost musical score in which a fixed sort of elements played their way up and down through the layers. By accident the rings left by a cup of tea on a drawing suggested organising the piece around two semi-circular areas of slightly different diameters. These began on the first floor providing the constant motif as they were cut up through the floors and roof. Where these circles crossed, a peculiar, almost row-boat shaped hole resulted and was mutated from floor to floor as structural beams and available floor space dictated.

In this project, now called *Office Baroque*, the disposition of spaces (large open offices near the ground, small interconnecting rooms toward the top) determined how the formal elements transformed from uninterrupted circular slices to shrapnel-like bits and pieces of the original form as they 'collided' with partitions and walls. Besides the surprise and disorientation this work stimulates, it creates an especially satisfying mental map or model to help the eye remember. *Office Baroque* is distinct from earlier projects by eluding what I call snapshot interpretation. This is a single characteristic view which one might find on a postcard or an art documentation. There is a sad irony in this. Although the project is in a prime location with many people hovering just outside the locked doors, the only way to get a comprehensive idea of the work is to wander through from top to bottom inside. I suppose it will be another esoteric hidden work in the history of inaccessible projects.'[9]

Notes

1 Interview with Gordon Matta-Clark by Donald Wall, 'Gordon Matta-Clark's Building Dissections', *Arts Magazine*, March 1976, pp74-79.
2 Gordon Matta-Clarke, notebook
3 Gordon Matta-Clark reported by Donald Wall in 'Gordon Matta-Clark's Building Dissections', *Arts Magazine*, March 1976, pp74-79. Reprinted in *Matta-Clark*, (exhib cat), International Cultureel Centrum, Antwerp, September 1977, pp40-41.
4 Interview with Matta-Clark in *Matta-Clark*, (exhib cat), International Cultureel Centrum, Antwerp, September 1977, pp9-10.
5 Alice Aycock in conversation with Joan Simon in *Gordon Matta-Clark: A Retrospective*, (exhib cat), Museum of Contemporary Art, Chicago, 1985, p33.
6 Horace Solomon in conversation with Joan Simon in *Gordon Matta-Clark: A Retrospective, op cit*, p73
7 Interview with Matta-Clark in *Matta-Clark, op cit*, p10.
8 Interview with Matta-Clark in *Matta-Clark*, (exhib cat), International Cultureel Centrum, Antwerp, 1977, p11.
9 *ibid*.

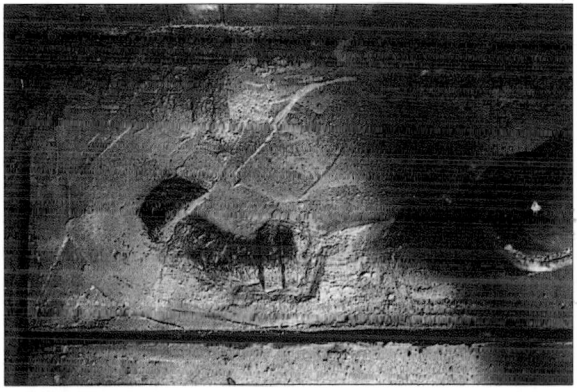
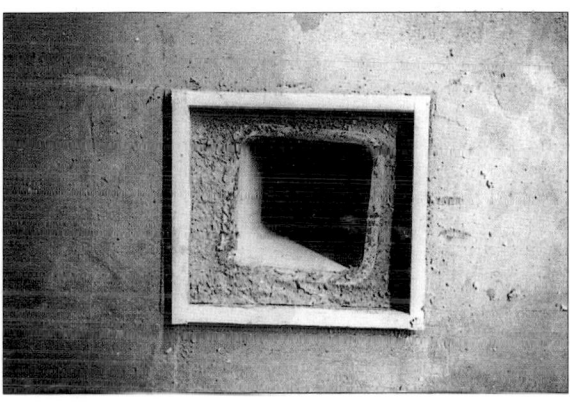

LEFT. Time Well, *1971*

awake state. Most of the light or colour that we experience is subtractive, in the sense that it is coming off a surface. We see light generally as something that illuminates other things. I'm interested in the *thingness* of light and the object-quality of perception. I want the actual act of seeing to be the object of attention.

CF: *To what extent did your fascination with light come about through living in Los Angeles?*

JT: Los Angeles is a place where you do experience light quite a bit but then you also experience it in England and Ireland. You can find some pretty impressive maritime skies there, different skies to California, grey skies, serious skies. But I think the experience of living in Los Angeles has more to do with how one looks at art. Los Angeles is a place that has no taste. It's not like San Francisco or Boston. We don't have the same restrictions that you do in Europe, in terms of what art is and what it is not. This may also have something to do with the experience of going to the moon. No one had been to the moon before so we had to figure out how to do it. The same thing happened in art. We had to make up our own rules. In the end however the market is a big determinant. To make a living from selling this work is very difficult. People want to know what they own. What do you tell them? That they own the light that is passing through, and the blue sky? It is difficult to assign a value to these things. To some degree there is a joy in that fact. This is work that makes a *thingness* of perception and a *thingness* of light.

CF: *How has the experience of flying your own plane affected your perception of light, colour and space? Has it brought about an interest in the physical sensation of weightlessness?*

JT: To some degree flying becomes the seat in my studio, because the light and colour and the open air, the phenomena of weather and the changes of light in the atmosphere is what I have to look at as source material. So you get a front row seat by flying yourself, and that's been very important. It also has to do with the idea of journey and the primacy of *experience* over the *object* of experience. In small aircraft I enjoy weightlessness as a positive feeling but it is not a concern in my work. People talk about my spaces as being endless, but they are actually finite spaces. What you realise is that to see to the end of the space you have to look *through* something and that *thing* is light happening in space. I feel that there is a physicality given to the substance of light. We have a strong primal relationship to light. When you stare into a fire, for example, you enter into a kind of non-thinking state, or at least a non-thinking-in-words state. This is only diminished by associative thought. Artists have had a fascination with light for a long time. I'm not only thinking of paintings which are *about* light. In certain Celtic, Egyptian and even south-western Indian sites there is a working with light events *into* space. This is something that pre-dates easel painting.

CF: *To what extent is your work the result of re-search into the psychology of perception? Do you want your pieces to retain an element of magic and mystery?*

JT: I don't think my work has anything to do with scientific research. I'm more interested in the questions than the answers, which can destroy the mystery. I don't use light as a scientist. I use it in a very irresponsible, reckless way, as artists should. Some of the purposes of science have been subverted by the military. Even the ceremony marking the first landing on the moon was turned over to militarists. An event such as this should have been choreographed by Martha Graham and Merce Cunningham.

CF: *How do you calculate light in a given space?*

JT: Each site presents different problems. I work with diagrams to order a construction. I also work with models but the qualities of light don't scale up easily. In the same way sound is difficult to scale. In the end I work mainly on site.

CF: *In your comments about light, you have said that 'for something so powerful, situations for its felt presence are fragile.' Have you been inspired by the light and space in any particular buildings?*

JT: I am interested in the *hypethral* space in Greek architecture. There is some controversy about this. I don't think it was ever intended to be covered by anything other than the sky which is brought down to the top of the space. I look at buildings in terms of the experience of entering them. The places that most command my attention are large civic spaces that are no longer used, such as Monte Albán (the temple city of the Zapotecs situated on a mountain near Oaxaca in Mexico). The experience of entering such a space is just the experience of the space itself. The way in which light fills the spaces of Gothic cathedrals is also very amazing. I'm interested in making the spaces that we're familar with in dreams and in the imagination. I want space to be experienced with the eyes open. Only when light is reduced considerably can feeling move out of the eyes into the space. My work is about reducing the loudness of light so that we feel its presence.

CF: *Were your first experiments with light projections inspired, perhaps, by the simple effects of a shaft of sunlight entering a room through a window and being projected onto a white wall?*

JT: Yes. This is not an art of complication.

CF: *Merleau-Ponty has written that the senses communicate with each other 'in the general action of being in the world.' He describes the experience of visual perception when 'suddenly the sensible takes possession of my gaze, and I surrender a part of my body, even my whole body, to this particular manner of vibrating and filling space known as blue or red.'[2] Would you like to comment on this?*

JT: Merleau-Ponty was a very significant phenomenologist in studies of perception. I am interested in the kind of seeing where the field of vision is inextricably entered by seeing it, so you become a part of it. I want you to see *your* seeing. In the Dark Spaces the object of perception exists only as a stimulus to seeing.

CF: *Is silence essential to this experience?*

JT: True silence, as John Cage noted, is unattainable. But you can have relative silences that allow you to attend to important things that are not generally seen as being important. My work is made for one person. I like the solitary experience. Standing alone at night, perceiving the Roden Crater and the moon and stars, you really feel the vastness of the universe and yourself entering into it. It's not an experience that diminishes the self.

CF: *Have you been influenced by Mark Rothko?*

JT: Rothko's work was strongly about light and has been a powerful influence. This is also true of Monet whose work interests me, particularly his haystacks. The haystack is the object of perception but what Monet is really looking at is the light. I have also been influenced by Cézanne's paintings of Mont Sainte Victoire. You really see how it was perceived under different light conditions and at different times of the day. I would just like to stand you in front of Mont Sainte Victoire at the times when you could not miss the desired seeing. I want that direct seeing that is *your* seeing and doesn't come through me.

CF: *Do you think about your Shallow-Space Constructions – in which rectangles of coloured light are perceived in a space that seems to have no depth – in terms of 'light paintings'?*

JT: I have a painter's eye in three dimensions. The Shallow-Space Constructions deal with a three-dimensional space that is perceived in two dimensions and also with the idea of the penetration of vision, entering a space with seeing and plumbing it only with vision.

CF: *Do you like to play perceptual games?* In *Rayzor*, as shown at the Anthony d'Offay Gallery in 1991, I take a wall and I dematerialise it using white gauze and light. The light becomes more of a thing than the actual wall which no longer looks like a thing. This has to do with my sense of humour.

CF: *Giuseppe Panza has described his first experience of your work, when he entered a room in which 'the walls were almost disappearing in the whiteness of the space which contained nothing but light'.*[3] *Is it your intention to disorientate the viewer in space?*

JT: I dematerialise the physical walls and I materialise the things that we tend to think of as being intangible. I don't intend to disorientate the viewer in space. I want to give primacy to things that tend not to be consciously seen. We're so attached to the notion of art as treasure. This is not interesting to me.

CF: *Can you explain how you change the perception of a given space, using both natural and artificial light, in your Wedgeworks and Space-Division Pieces?*

JT: In the Wedgeworks I like to go from the translucent to the transparent, to actually see the change, to see the physicality and then to see it dissolve. In the Space-Division Pieces you actually feel the tangibility of the light to the extent that you almost want to touch it. I had an interesting experience in the Stedelijk Museum in Amsterdam when I was asked to take a group of very young school children through the exhibition and to answer their questions. Looking at a light projection one of the children wanted to know how much it weighed. Another child wanted to know how, if you put your hand through the opening in one of the apertures, you could then wash the light off your hand. These were the first two questions I had to answer and it went on from there! The work is made for this other way of seeing things but I was actually unprepared for questions totally coming from that other arena. These children saw what I wanted them to see in a very matter of fact way.

CF: *Yves Klein wrote that 'blue has no dimensions, it is beyond dimensions,' and Kandinsky wrote that red is an expanding colour that pulses forward towards the viewer. Have you conducted your own research into the effects of colour on the senses?*

JT: Absolutely. I was not influenced directly by Kandinsky or Klein, although I enjoy their approach to colour. It's actually possible to reconstruct vision using only blue-violet, red and green. You can reconstruct the entire spectrum using these three additive-light colours. I often mix red and blue. I am interested in both the physical limits of perception and the unconscious limits of perception that come about through habitual ways of thinking. For example we tend to think of red as a hot colour and blue as a cold colour. But white heat is actually hotter than red heat. In the same way tungsten light which looks a red-yellow colour is cooler than if you excite xenon which is a colourless gas, a higher frequency in the blue spectrum and similar to daylight. This kind of perception is something we have learned, it's not how things actually are, it's how we've decided to see them. I play with these limits of perception. I want people to see what is really going on.

CF: *'As I contemplate the blue of the sky . . . I do not possess it in thought, or spread out towards it some idea of blue such as might reveal the secret of it, I abandon myself to it, and plunge into this mystery.'*[4] *In the light of this statement from the* Phenomenology of Perception, *how do you want the viewer to experience your Skyspaces?*

JT: I certainly want that feeling of vision and intensity to be there, particularly at the change of night into day and day into night. I want you to realise that the sky is not something out there, away from us. Rather, we are dwellers at the bottom of the ocean of air. We create the colour and shape of the sky. It does not exist outside the self. We can enter it and plumb it with vision and we can change the perception of the sky. We can change its colour with the light inside the space. I'm interested in how we form this world outside ourselves or what we believe to be outside ourselves.

CF: *Do you experience the passage of time in the Skyspace?*

JT: I think you do. My work certainly involves time.

Sometimes it has more to do with a feeling of timelessness. We construct time. It doesn't exist in the same way that light does and so I think this idea of the existence of time is a very interesting one.

CF: *Giuseppe Panza has described the experience of viewing one of your Sky Windows, a rectangular aperture cut into the top of a white wall and opening onto the sky. As the sun set the opening changed colour, from blue to orange, through to violet and finally black. The colours seemed to be painted onto the surface of the wall.*

JT: Yes. I want you to come away with the realisation that space is not an empty void. You are looking into a medium that has physicality. Its existence has as much primacy as ours.

CF: *You have said that you are interested in 'the invisible light' that is perceived in the mind.*

JT: I am interested in this imaginative seeing that we experience with the eyes closed. I'm interested in where the seeing from within meets the seeing from without, that is how imagined seeing enters into the outside world, how we actually create what we see. The outward is driven by the inward to such a degree that it's difficult to separate the two. In the Dark Spaces I'm also interested in the fact that you carry with you the images from outside as after-images. It can take two to three minutes before they dissolve. Then the process of projecting the imagined seeing onto the outside stimuli begins. What is outside triggers off this imagined seeing.

CF: *Can you explain your holograms?*

JT: I am interested in looking at holograms simply as light, as light *being* light. The four holograms I made for the Hayward are analogous to the passage of the weather front. Each one is a plane of light. The first plane exists in front of the glass, the second is on the glass, the third is into the wall and the fourth comes out at an angle like a Wedgework. I am interested not in light used to depict something solid, but in the hologram seen merely as light.

CF: *And your Perceptual Cells?*

JT: This work comes out of my early studies in perceptual psychology. I am trying to recreate situations that I have found delight in. You can enter them and discover the same things that I did. I am very interested in the charged spaces that we have, for example the telephone box. When you enter one, say in a busy train station, you're not so much in that space as in contact with the other space that you are through to. We have these spaces that are strangely separated from normal space. For example, when a child is naughty and is made to stand in the corner of a room, what's the big deal? It has to do with how society has psychologically determined that space.

CF: *Your works in Arizona, Israel and Ireland seem to be uniting the earth and sky. Is this your intention?*

JT: Yes. I am interested in the interaction of the earth and sky, in looking up from the familiar human landscape into the sky. I also have made works where you look down into water and see the reflection of the sky and the movement of the clouds. I

want to involve the sky in the interior and near landscape. I like the idea of tending the sky, colouring and shaping it. In each site I am working with local materials, sand of all colours, as in the Painted Desert and the dry desert sky. There is a brilliance and clarity to the skies in Arizona. Here you have the dry reds of the desert.

CF: *How did the Painted Desert in Arizona get its name and how are you reshaping the Roden Crater?*

JT: The name comes from the fact that the colours are so amazing out here. You can fill these little bottles with coloured sands from the Painted Desert – blue sands, moon-green sands, black, red and purple sands. Even from the Roden Crater you can see brilliant reds, pale greens and purples. Different areas have different colours, depending on the geological formations. This is an area of exposed geology. When it rains it's just like when you take a rock and you dip it into water. The colours become more fully saturated. The dramatic light effects have a lot to do with the angle of the sun that changes during the day so that things that are seen in a purple haze suddenly reveal themselves as being very brilliant in colour. Also the bottoms of the clouds will often be coloured by the sunlight on the desert. You can have pink on the underside of the clouds, then the white cloud and the blue sky. It can be a very beautiful and subtlely changing show.

I am making spaces that will be empowered by sunlight, starlight and moonlight. There are very precise alignments for certain light and astronomical events to happen, but many interesting events come from the cloud being between the source of light and the earth, or from snow that is on the ground, underlighting the spaces in fascinating ways. There are events which we know will happen, but we cannot predict exactly when they will happen. I make these spaces so that they themselves see. I put things in motion and then the crater makes its own show. There is a basic framework but within that framework there is quite a bit of change which I have no control over.

This was originally an area of grassland and recently there has been a drive to replant these grasses. I'm involved in that. The interior of the bowl is just grassland, very similar to how portions of it were before, as you can see in early photographs. The yellow grass intensifies the blue of the sky because they are complimentary colours. The blue is already made stronger because of the bowl shape which eliminates the white haze seen at the horizon.

The interior of the crater is shaped specifically to shape our perception of the sky. It makes this vaulting effect or doming over the top of the crater. The spaces that I make are like eyes in the sense that they are themselves seeing, they give shape to the perception.

CF: *To what extent have you been influenced by the Hopi and Navajo Indians?*

JT: I would like to be more influenced by them. They have interesting ways of seeing things. They talk about the star groupings as celestial beings. They have a familiarity with the sky that we have lost but which I would like to rediscover. They have spaces that are oriented to celestial events, specifically to the winter solstice because of the planting cycles.

CF: *How are you incorporating astronomical events into the Roden Crater?*

JT: I am assisted by Dr Richard Walker of the Naval Observatory in Flagstaff. If I know where the light is coming from and when it will be there, then I can do something with it. The light projections inside the crater will come about naturally, like light entering a window and being projected onto a wall. In the north space you can see clouds projected onto the floor during the day, as with a camera obscura, and at night the space is related to the northern procession of the equinoxes, a 26,000-year cycle. So we are sometimes dealing with that kind of time scale. In the Painted Desert you feel geological time. Within that I am making spaces that engage celestial events, so to some degree the music of the spheres is being played out in light. I am also using the solar radiation by putting black volcanic sand in front of some of the openings which produces a shimmering quality in the space, similar to the effect seen when heat rises from highway tarmac. In general, each space has a night aspect and a day aspect. The general quality is a mixing of the ambient light of the space that creates a sense of atmosphere, filling the space. This is similar to the quality of light as seen in the Space Division Pieces. This sense is occasionally interrupted by some celestial event which creates an image like that in a camera obscura, or a pinhole camera, or just light coming through a window. This imaged event obliterates the sense of atmosphere and for a short period of time, say four minutes, the space calls attention to seldom noticed events by isolating them and occluding almost all other light.

CF: *Will sound play a part in the Roden Crater?*

JT: I am interested in the way in which *light* inhabits a space. I want to do this with sound as well. One space deals with the sound of Grand Falls which flows strongly in the springtime, when the snow melts, about five miles from the crater. This desert waterfall occasionally has flows that exceed Niagara Falls. The space is filled with water in which the sound of the waterfall is projected. You can only enter by going under water and then coming up inside it. The temperature inside the space is like that in a cave. There is another space where we have used radio astronomy to record the sound of the sky – the big sounds of the sun and Jupiter. You have to be under water to hear the sounds.

CF: *Do you think it will be possible to capture the experience of the Roden Crater on film?*

JT: No. The only thing to film is the Roden Crater itself from a mile or two away. Once you are inside it you are just looking into space. There is nothing to focus on, no place to point the camera.

CF: *You have said that you are interested in 'the actuality rather than thoughts about the cosmos.'*

Yes. I am interested in seeing the sky right in front of you, no longer *out there*. I want the cosmos to be actually felt. I am concerned with actual experience.

An exhibition of James Turrell's work will be held at the Hayward Gallery, London from 8 April – 27th June 1993

Notes

1   Maurice Merleau-Ponty, 'Sense Experience', *Phenomenology of Perception*, translated from the French by Colin Smith, Routledge, London, 1962, p207, p216.

2   *ibid*, p214

3   Giuseppe Panza, 'Beyond the Frame', interview with Clare Farrow, New Museology, *Art & Design*, London, 1991, pp50-61.

4   Merleau-Ponty, *op cit* p214.

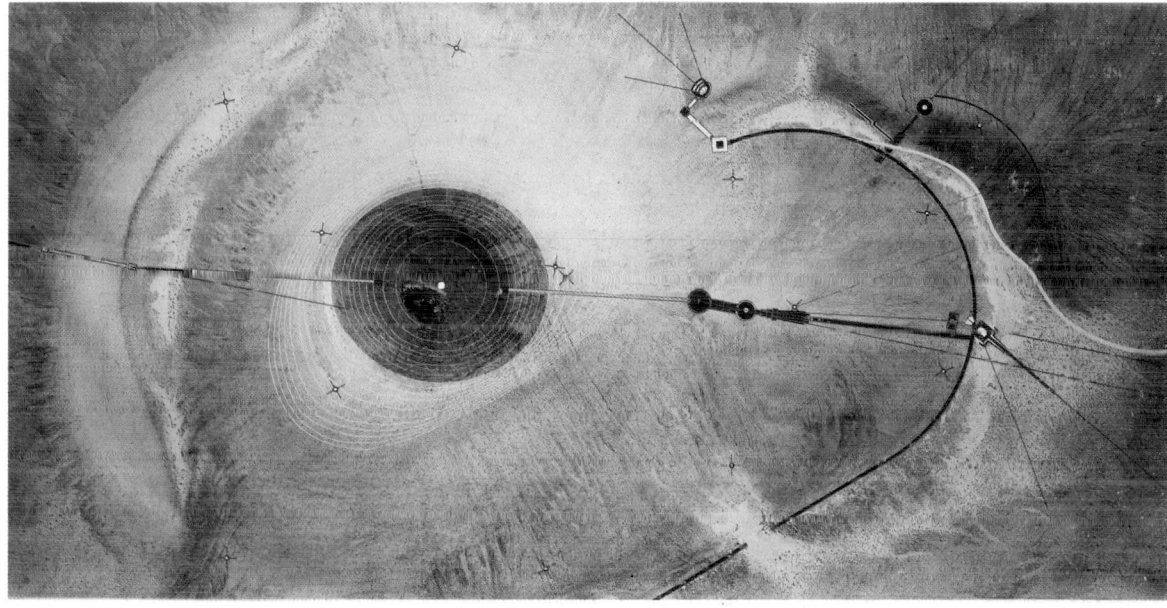

LEFT: Negative Site Plan, 1992, beeswax, photograph emulsion, oil pastel, acrylic, ink and graphite with dry mounted vellum on mylar

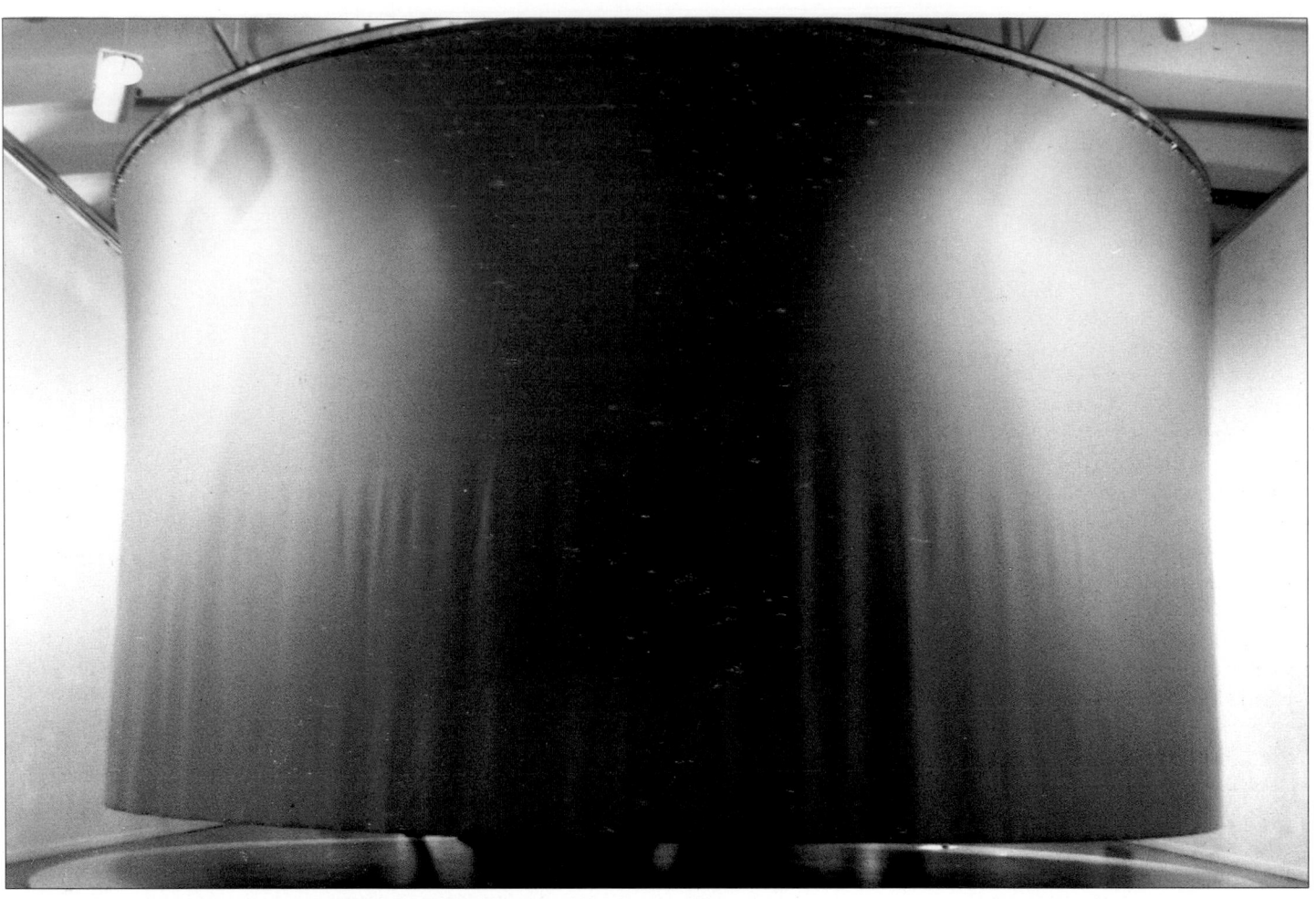
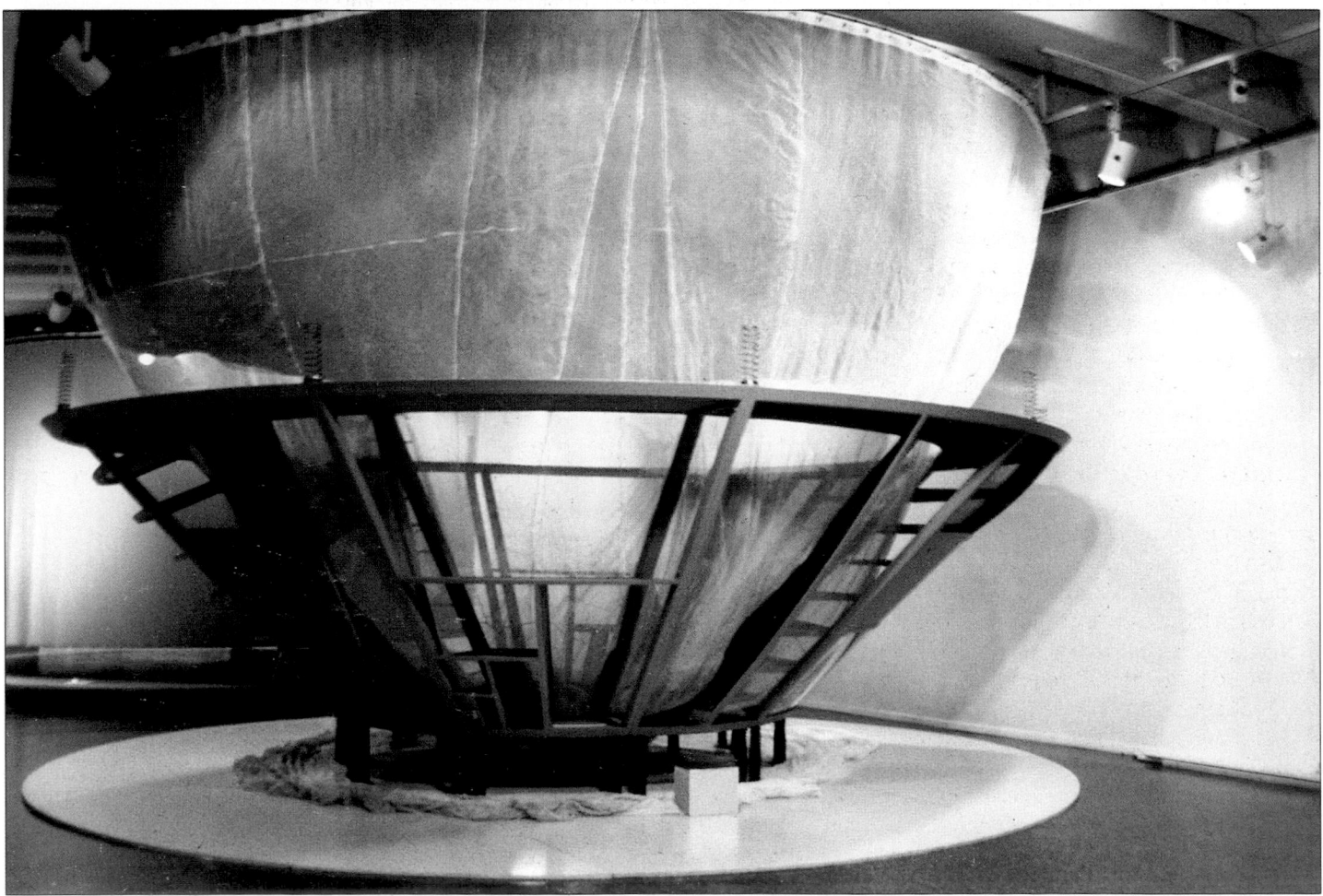

JEAN-FRANÇOIS LYOTARD
RESERVES OF SPATIAL EVENTS
Arakawa and Madeline Gins

They have said what they mean, they have written it, and are showing it. Is it then only possible to say what they did not mean to say? It is after all the task of commentary to add an affect to the one that inhabits the works, secretly. When left to itself, the work perishes, if it is not transmitted and taken up again. To transmit it and take it up again is not to claim to translate it, to express, or even to interpret its meaning. From your sealed silence, something comes to me. From mine, something will go. What is this thing that is not the same in you and in me, that is always singular, and yet gives rise to that one and age-old enterprise called art? It is a thing that is always our own in the other, that is only at home in the other. You welcome the other such that he is at home in you. But in his own home, no one knows him, not even himself. It is thus that I will welcome the work of Arakawa-Gins (AG) exhibited in Tokyo.

In the other – to whom the Tokyo installation offers its hospitality – it is impossible not to recognise the presence of Duchamp. In the first place, by the insistence of the secret. And like the *Etant Donnés*, the AG exhibition is the architectural recasting of a motif already explored through paintings and drawings. In both cases, the entire work opens and closes as a vast painted diptych. On one side, there is the work in two dimensions, the transparencies, the blanks: for Duchamp, the *Large Glass* with all its *parerga*, drawings, details, sketches and edges; for AG, the work in pencil and acrylic of the 60s, the large paintings of the 70s and 80s, and the preparatory drawings of the 80s. On the other side, there is the work in three-dimensions, the sculptures, the architectures, the installations: here, the *Bridge*, the *Tentative Constructed Plans*, the *Sites*, the panels of *To Not to Die*, *Envelope Hall*; there, *Etant Donnés*.

Elsewhere, I have tried to show that this last piece proceeds from the same sort of gesture as *La Mariée*. In the same way, the Tokyo installation takes up again, in three-dimensions, the problematic that underlies the large panels of 1975-85.

Why, in both cases, is the secret question, first addressed to the surfaces, transcribed into a so-called 'real' space-time? No doubt the question becomes more complicated with the addition of another dimension to the medium of inscription. It becomes more explicit; it is modalised in another way; it extends its reach to the everyday, inhabitable world. But in so doing, the secret is all the better guarded. The installation offers the visitor the evidence of what is there: it looks familiar. When glued to the door of the *Etant Donnés*, the eye is infinitely more likely to misunderstand the scene it is viewing than when, lost and dumbfounded, it comes up against the incomprehensible *Glass*. I believe that the visitors to the Museum of Modern Art in Tokyo will move about naturally, at first, between *Bridge*, *Ubiquitous Site* and *Plans*, without feeling in any way perturbed by the anguish that haunts the installation. At the Padiglione of Milan, in 1984, they must have experienced total stupefaction when standing before the 15 metres long *Or Detail/of the Model/Hypostatising Distance* . . . an enormous enigma that makes one unsure of what one thinks and what one sees.

The trap set by the AG installation is, I think, even more perfect than the one set by Duchamp. The door of *Etant Donnés* acts like a screen; it reinforces one's curiosity, but it imposes the distance of voyeurism: one does not enter. The peep show thus plays on the two-dimensional barrier, and imposes a perverse *ascesis*. The AG installation, however, seems to require no *ascesis* of the body, no interruption of its spontaneous mobility. The visitor enters, comes and goes between the enclosures in his habitual way; he occupies spaces that seem inhabitable to him, climbs on the inclined planes, crawls under the rubber curtains, enjoys himself. The large paintings of around 1980 didn't allow him to resort to that natural defence: movement.

At least for the most part. For one could not help but walk along, draw near, or move away from these paintings. It would be important to study our movements before these large, flat works: how the shifts in our angle of vision, the changes in distance, the dance which is imposed on our body by those surfaces that deny it the *habitus* of depth, are like laughter – uncontrollable laughter. When it is overly restricted or restrained, depth bursts into movement. Agitation and laughter normally protect the life of the body and soul from something that is not quite sensed, infra-sensed or ultra-sensed. Monkeys before a Botticelli: they immediately look for what is behind, eager to make it resemble an object that is compatible with their customary ways of moving.

The body, immersed in a sensory world that is thought, by definition, to accord with what it can perceive and with its accommodating movements, encounters, in painting, a surface without depth. Painting immobilises the body, reminds it of the threat exercised on it by brute sensation, which it eludes by constructing its sphere of actions and perceptions.

What threat? A strange thing affects the body, having to do with *colour,* which the body cares nothing about. It is in fact strange that it can affect it so. And yet the body knows, thanks to the experience of painting, that it is constantly affected by colour, that it lives in a chromatic field and that, from the point of view of vision, it couldn't live without being affected by it. But, usually, this depends on its capacity to transform this affection into perceptions, recognitions, movements and actions. The painted panel, whatever its colours and disposition, eliminates this possibility. It doesn't open onto a perceptual-motor field simply because it has only two dimensions. It disturbs; it silences. It is uninhabitable. And its colour stops being a stimulus; it is just there; it asks nothing of the body. This proud indifference reminds our normally busied vision that it owes everything to colour, that it is dependant on it: without it, the eye would have nothing to see.

These banal reflections now allow us to approach the AG notion of 'cleaving'. Removing dimensions from objects (or adding them to them?) in a perceptual field has the effect of isolating them from the field while still maintaining them there. The properties of this object undergo a sort of moulting. They stop 'speaking' to the body the language of perception and of movement. They require of it an entirely different mode of being: the neutralisation of its competence as a living body; the acknowledgment that it is not suited to these properties when they are freed from three-dimensional space; the *liability* of the body to their very matter. This transformation is the *ascesis* of which I spoke; it is signaled by the dumbfoundedness and the stupefaction that announce the experience of cleaving. Sight is deprived of *its* colour; colour snatches eyes that are unprepared to see it. Seeing changes senses. The art of painting, namely the one at work in the large panels of Arakawa, consists in this mutation, where, at the same time, colour is separated (cleaved) from sight, and vision is stuck (cleaved) onto the 'colour' that causes sight to be. This colour 'before' colours is what, in AG's work, is named *blank.*

The AG installation in Tokyo seeks a mutation in space analogous to the mutation in colour that takes place in the painted panel. And just as two-dimensional painting requires an *ascesis* of sight with respect to the visible, three-dimensional installations, despite their familiar appearance, require an *ascesis* of the body with respect to the *inhabitable.*

As I have said, the visitors will certainly misunderstand at first the spatial property of the enclosures that are exhibited, just as the viewer of a painting initially focuses on what it 'represents' (in an imagined three-dimensional space). But they will quickly be amazed. These strange architectures are not inhabitable in the ordinary sense. It is difficult to keep on moving in an habitual way in these enclosures that have no perceptible finality. They seem to usher in – or into – nothing. The visitor, once he has entered them, soon no longer knows *where he is at.* A strange thing affects him, *having to do with space,* which has nothing to do with him, despite his first impression. A voiceless anguish mixed with a promise. Perhaps a laugh.

The same was true of the space of the *Etant Donnés,* as I have said. But there, one didn't enter; another place remained, located elsewhere. In the AG installation, the elsewhere is here; the cleavage is imminent; the door is open, we passed through it, it is that of the Museum of Modern Art of Tokyo; it is very 'real', unlike the Catalan portal of Duchamp, an improved ready-made with its symbolic function.

The lower part of the *Glass* is organised according to conventional rules of perspective. It imposes a three-dimensional reading of a two-dimensional medium, and that reading is that of males. Male-language appropriates space according to the lucid articulation of Euclidian geometry. But this well-regulated space is inhabited by another space, that of the upper part of the Glass, where the woman is floating, suspended, out of reach. The notes of the green and white boxes suggest that the figure of the *Mariée* is the projection onto the surface of the Glass of an n-dimensional form (where n is more than 3). The men thus remain bachelors. The door of the *Etant Donnés* condemns them in turn to voyeurism. The woman offered, on the other side, in the public garden, remains inaccessible. However, in both cases, the male-language and the woman-thing, which are absolutely heterogenous, are necessarily linked. One can't exist without the other. For articulated language and its logic of meaning engenders, in itself, the melancholy of its separation from things and the illusion of a meaning that is always eluding it. Thus sexual difference perfectly matches the *aporia* of cleaving: linking while separating. Which is the very notion of limit.

Arakawa and Gins write: 'Even when something seems to have been cut off from all the rest, still can it be seen in the end to have somehow adhered.' The same problematic is still at issue, though it is no longer man/woman, but dead/alive. The installation clearly states its stakes: 'to not to die', 'to elude mortality', 'to reverse destiny', where destiny consists in decline ('downhill'). The AG *différend* finds its 'place' between differentiation or complexity and de-differentiation or entropy; it opposes a very improbable state of energy with its most probable state. For living things, the conflict never ends, between the growth and the suppression of their powers, between their strange energy to start something new and the absolute asthenia of death.

One could precisely object to this presentation of the limit in AG's work, that it consists in a simple opposition between two terms, rather than in the *aporia* of a limit or of a cleaving. In order to accord the limit its true status, one must show that the promotion of complexity, in the exhibition and the practice of livable space, for example, is marked by a sort of invalidation of the motor functions of the body, through the aforementioned *ascesis*, that consists in the defection of sensory givens. And one must also show that the 'good' life of the organism, its well-being, the pleasure it derives from the space-time that surrounds it, implies the mortification of the capacity for inhabitation that remains unseen beyond. This will be examined later.

Now to finish with the Duchampian filiation of the work of AG, it is clear that despite the difference of inscription, the same principle is shared: for the *artistic* to emerge, the capacity of the mind-body must be exceeded. There is no work of art that does not summon our sensibility to its fright before its precariousness, to its terror. From this constitutive defeat, which he turns into castration, Duchamp draws his familiar conclusions: one never sees the thing bare; language remains celibate, that is to say tautological; perception, when it offers the promise of an elsewhere, is a trap; painting that believes in the visible is dumb; there is colour only when it is named. And if one must exceed something by the artistic act, it can only be language itself and by itself. Language must then be played against itself, with its own means, within its closure. If its claim to consistency is vain, then all its inconsistencies must be exposed: paralogisms, synonyms, homonyms, all the features that attest to the presence *in it* of the thing that it lacks and that which exceeds it.

For example, geometrical language, examining its presuppositions, discovers that it need not necessarily limit itself to the study of one, two, or three-dimensional spaces. Three+n-dimensional figures are, if not conceivable, at least workable. Duchamp inscribes this possibility in the art of space, in the name of sexual difference. Male-language can say of woman-thing that she is a three+n-dimensional figure. It is 'precise', yet it remains 'inaccurate-precise' because it is clearly articulated, inaccurate because the n cannot be determined. Art is language phlegmatically experiencing the symptoms of its separation.

In Tokyo, we see and hear something quite different. AG's work doesn't enclose itself in language in order to discover opportunities for an 'irony of affirmation', as Duchamp used to say. The sensory world is of course questioned, but it is not rejected as an illusion. It is solicited on two accounts: it promises more life, and it threatens death.

At the beginning of *Tentative Constructed Plan,* there is the sense that natural perception actualises only a negligible part of visibility. The visual harbours the promise of visions still unseen. The tentative 'constructed plan' wants to offer vision 'perceptual landing sites' and opportunities of 'engaging', which our perceptual-motor habits eliminate. 'Engaging a perceptual landing site and landing on the site and having it become perceptually alive are all the same.' I stress 'alive': it is about an awakening; the plan is built to give life to, and to keep watch over that which lies dormant in the

perceptual, beneath the perceptible. How can one manoeuvre to obtain this breakthrough into the sensory world and this deployment of spatial possibilities? 'By means of the continual assigning of a group of numerous surrounding or accompanying other planes to each new plane upon which the site must be recognised as also being situated, an initial sense of ubiquitous site might be arrived at.' One takes the constitutive oppositions of inhabitable cubic space: before/behind, above/beneath, right/left; and to each pair, the other 3 pairs are applied. A strange space then arises: *forebackleftright, forebackupdown, forebackforeback, foreupleftright, foredownbackup* etc, which is reminiscent of Cubism or of the repeated strategy of inserting the shape of a curve into all of its segments, thus generating the fractal line.

This procedure must not be assimilated to the Duchampian usage of the n-dimensional. Here, the 'complexifying' of sites and their ubiquitousness does not remove them from perception. The field of the visible is extended into the visual field without ceasing to be visible. And the visual is potential visibility. This operation is not mental, or linguistic; the cleaving operates on the given itself. Far from freeing the eye and the body from sensory depth, the 'building of the plan' engages them even more. On all its sides, a site opens onto a labyrinth of sites. It thus reveals its power to situate. The *situation,* in its active sense, thus appears as the fact of the site. The site is a situating enclosure. And the body, in turn, becomes a site among the sites, in as much as it situates. The 'world', a set of sites, becomes energy-matter again, creating its own space-time.

Could one argue that these enclosures, that carve out their depths and their dwellings, are more mental than real? AG's work in its entirety would respond that this opposition is futile. Sensory reality is also mental. But this is due to an invalid *mens* (I would argue, from authority, but perhaps arguably, that Kant, in the end, also confuses sensibility and imagination). 'It may never be possible to ascertain whether perceptual landing sites, posited here for heuristic purposes, actually exist.' The assertion of reality is a problem of cognition, not of perception, and even less of art.

This strategy of opening onto the life of material space might evoke an ideology of conquest. Unexploited energies are seized upon and put to work. Only a hurried visitor could think that. When I attended the mounting of the *Bridge* in Williamstown in October of 1989, I was struck by just the opposite. This *Bridge of Reversible Destiny is* not a device for extracting or exploiting new resources; it does not lead euphorically to more life. It is itself a meshing of planes and of lines, seemingly devoid of any *function.* Its delicate complexity produces rather a feeling of anxiety, as if it had fallen from another planet where perceptive differentiation was keener than ours. It is useless to run around these enclosures in an attempt to master them; one is outdone.

'Sky ceasing to be sky becomes ubiquitous site, and possibly too, phantom (second) tentative constructed plan. The perceiver, when negotiating the various declivities and acclivities of the surface's numerous inclines, becomes increasingly fearful of coming to some harm, switches off automatic and onto alert'. *Fearful of coming to some harm,* perception disconnects, the alarm goes off.

AG's work is not colonialist, nor is it experimentalist. It is tentative in that it is *timid*, imbued with ancient *time*: exposure being to the danger of perception rather than a statement addressed to a public. Struck by the ubiquitousness of the site, the subject risks losing its reference to itself and the monopoly of its point of view. The inhabitable starts to live off itself and to proliferate from site to site. The fragile 'balance' of the subject-object relation is undone in a play of planes that echo off each other without ever stabilising. The intoxication of space provoked by AG's work awakens in the viewer the fear of being observed. He is no longer the miniature-god whose seeing makes form out of matter; he is but one moment in the transformative process of space-time-energy, one of those moments when matter is reflected onto itself. 'We want to build tentative constructed plans that will one day become the observer and not just the observed.'

Art would not exist if it didn't remind us of the disaster that looms in the slightest sensation. I would see no colour if the energy, not yet coloured by any human sense – *blank*, what Klee called 'the grey' – a substance to which I am blind, didn't affect me. I'd hear no sound if something inaudible weren't given to be filtered by my hearing. Art awakens the anguish of this sort of subordination, the terror of owing the life of the senses to a power that this life knows nothing about and which nevertheless sustains it. Painting reminds the eye of its blindness, music the ear of its deafness, architecture reminds the body that inhabits it that it is naked and paralysed in the desert. Duchamp transcribes this truth, 'transfers' it, he would say, into sexual difference and masks it's 'ironism'. AG's work tentatively attempts to be its witness, at the risk of madness.

Such is the secret of *cleaving,* as I have said: to separate and to link together. Every relation, every linking, is the promise of an additional determination (*positioning*) and at the same time the experience of nothingness. Any given term, before it is connected again with another term – sight to the visible not yet seen, thought to another thought unthought – is not yet anything and remains dead in its separation. But even as the relation to the other term is established, it will *still* be saying to the first that it is nothing in itself, that it exists only in this state of dependancy, that it lives only when nourished by the other, and that its survival hangs on the arbitrariness of an unknown 'presence'. This threat of dying is never overcome.

Cut off is an adhering; but belonging is the mode of abandonment. In French, *partage* says both in one word, as does to *cleave:* one shares with, one is without. The relation to the self obeys the same contradictory law: one is shared with/from oneself, *fromwithinoneself.*

If the AG installation in Tokyo emanates an almost sacred silence, it is because it touches upon the untouchable, the transcendance of a spatiality immanent to space, the uninhabitable in the *habitus,* the invisible *blank* in colours.

This secret of *cleaving* was exposed in two-dimensions in the works in pencil and acrylic of the 60s. Among them was S*tretchable Labyrinth,* 1962 that anticipates the extensible or tensible labyrinth that is the 1991 installation. And that now is a component of the latter as one of its 'total parts', according to the rule of repetition already mentioned. The installation as a whole is a ubiquitous site, a grouping that is visual rather than visible, striated by cleavages. I am not refering to the *walls* that circumscribe the rooms of the Museum, for they have to do with the dividing up of space that governs Western architecture. The separation they establish between the inside and the outside seems unequivocal.

It is the *inner walls* of the sites that are the true 'dividers'. I picture them as analogous to those of a Japanese dwelling, *screenvalves* rather than *walls.* As a component of a 'temporarily built plan', the screenvalve exposes and hides a voluminousness that can spread, stretch and flee all around.

As for *Bridge,* it is a sort of model sequence of the perceptual labyrinth that is being sought. It has the threatening gleefulness of something that comes together and falls apart in an unexpected way. *Blank* frightens and causes jubilation. I use the word *sequence*, but it is inaccurate. The implications of AG's work on temporality should be examined here. Sequence refers to diachrony, to a time that is organised as a succession.

But if the bridge does indeed have as its purpose to suggest an inversion of destiny, where complexity is bound to be reduced to something less complex and more probable (death), then this inversion requires an inversion of the perception of the bridge. This perceptual inversion does not consist in going back in time, in crossing the bridge again in the other direction, but in grasping all at once its beginning as an end and its end as a beginning, and thus in eliminating both one and the other as such. The bridge is the representation of a cleaved spatiality that is potentially extensible and that is given in a single instant. This instant is not a moment in a sequence, nor is it a consequence. It is the event. The event is not destined to die, but its consequences are. The event is an apparition. Birth is an event because it is a beginning. As a beginning of a reality, the child's reality is always more complex and more unpredicatable than that of its genitor Σ, since the newly born derives from the *cleaving* (*partage* in both senses) of the genetic codes of each parent. Yet this birth is only the advent of a living being, that is in a binary opposition with its death to come, as one is to zero. And in this way, birth does not avoid death. Quite the contrary. But the cleaved relation that sustains the *Bridge* is more complex, because it does not lie inscribed within the course of life. The beginning and the end of the bridge are perceived in one go, as we were saying. But also each porous screenvalve that makes up the bridge both opens and closes the passage between the adjacent enclosures. It is thus, in itself, beginning and end, like the event. Not an end in the sense of a death at the end of the road, but as the event that disappears at the same time as its appears. All the elements of the bridge, and the bridge as a whole, 'exist', one might say, only according to the elusive temporality of the not-yet-already no longer. It is then not enough to say, as has just been said, that birth is an event because it is the beginning of something. One has to say that the event is, like death *and* birth, one instant of the temporal series that has no place in the series, since it has no before, like birth, and no after, like death.

It is not only the habitual space of perception that the AG installation works out and surpasses, but also time, the successive duration expended by sight as its scans the field of visibility. To not to die is to die to the time of death.

But these formulations are too filled with *pathos*. An Asian, nurtured in the Zen or Tao tradition, will recognise a familiar *ascesis* in AG's enterprise. The soul-body will methodically loose itself in order to escape *dharma*, the sequence of life-death Awakening, *satori*, the event *par excellence*, can only come about as a consequence of this *ascesis*. And in at least one of the Zen traditions (Sôtô), as in the work of AG, the price to pay is not the abandonment of the sensory world and the escape into mental nothingness. It is rather knowing how to elude, in the sensory world, the *appearance* of perception and how to expose oneself to the enigma of *apparition*. In this school of sensation, there is very little *pathos*. It is the West that adds pathos to perceptual *ascesis*, because it is forced to shatter the fundamental presuppositions of its mode of thought, the *ego*, the objectivity of the perceived world, the conflict between their respective powers.

The same serenity emanates from the matter that is involved in art. It is not the material that what we call the creative act works upon. Nor is it a power awaiting its final form. It is rather of the order of the impalpable energy to which contemporary physics reduces matter. And the work of art is like a reserve of energy concealed in the guise of an object in the sensory world. As such an object, institutions preserve and circulate it within their symbolic networks, as a cultural object, an object of discursive definition, a message exchanged between interlocutors, endowed with value by the commu-

nity. It thus enters into history, into the flow of consecutive time, it can be inscribed within series of influences, of effects, within contexts.

But the secret that the work imparts but never reveals comes from an immaterial matter that lies within it, that doesn't last and doesn't age, and that is non-sensory. It is the visible, audible trace of a gesture (*miburi* as Koji Takahashi suggests) of this matter and in this matter. And this gesture isn't itself perceptible, it allows for perception; it is not situated within the space-time of perception, it is itself situating, situation, as is an event. This gesture is the truth of the work of art, beauty, sublimity, that lasts throughout the ages and cannot die. Apparition does not depend on the flow of appearances. It depends on a site being offered to immaterial matter in such a way that it leaves its trace, as it instantly precipitates into an art-object, no longer recognisable.

It is in this way that the *Tentative Constructed Plan is* tentative: fearfully offered to the *blank* as a landing site. But what will have landed will make us forget *blank*, beneath the colours and the enclosures. This gesture doesn't express itself; it doesn't speak; *in-fans*, it operates a non-sensitive sensorium, *Infant*.

Painting is in search of a gesture that will allow the material power of seeing, itself invisible, to inscribe its trace in the visible. In the same way, architecture seeks to transfer into inhabitable space a power of habitation that is not itself inhabitable. This art cannot offer human beings any *topos* where they might live and be sheltered, that is to say, where they might escape from this elsewhere. One will be at home in the AG installation, and one will inhabit it, only in as much as the other, as inhabitable spatial matter, is at home in it, for one instant. This body is enveloped by the strange space; it is not packed into it. It is rather traversed or transversed by the power to embrace ('container') that is to architecture what *blank* is to the art of painting. This power makes the volumes flee into one another and out of one another; it reverses symmetries: *Reverse Symmetry Transverse Envelope Hall*. For one instant, the body, the everyday body, the body of the *habitus*, is exposed to the uninhabitable.

I admire the *excellence* of the titles and subtitles of AG's work. They are different – again in the same way – from the titles and subtitles of Duchamp, that are and can only be plays on words, tricks performed by language on itself. If collected, the AG titles and texts surrounding the Tokyo exhibition could be entitled as were the Dogen treatises of the 13th century: *Shôbôgenzô*, visual reserve of events in their exactness. Dogen writes that this reserve is *kokû*, air-empty, what here has been called matter.

The quotations are extracts from: Arakawa and Madeline Gins, 'The Tentative Constructed Plan as an Intervening Device (for a Reversible Destiny)', type script, 1991.

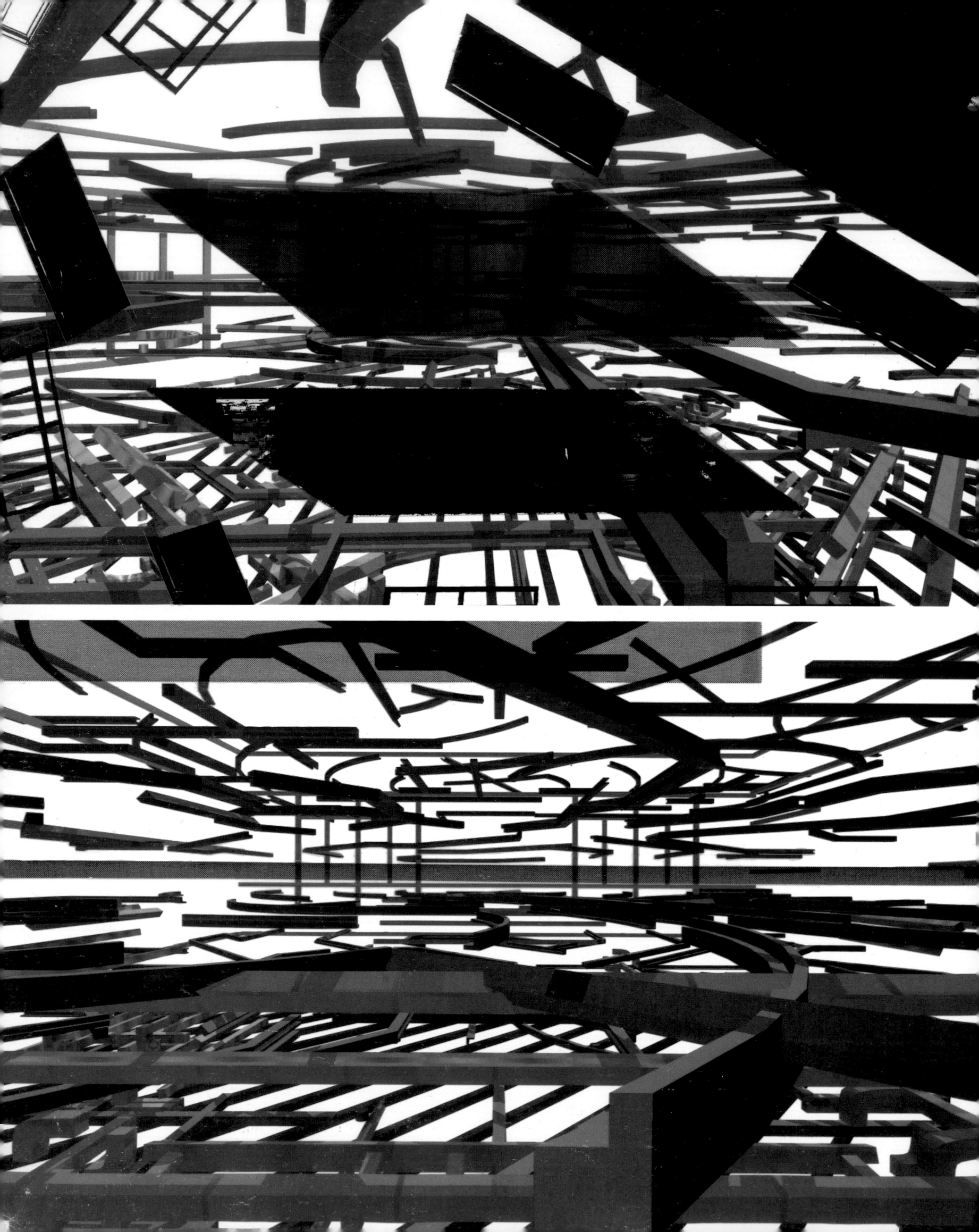

ARAKAWA AND MADELINE GINS
LANDING SITES/THE END OF SPACETIME

THE CONCEPT OF SPACETIME HAS NO EX-PLANATORY POWER IN REGARD TO THE BODY AND SURROUNDING EVENTS AND SHOULD THEREFORE BE REPLACED BY THE MORE BODILY ORIENTED AND THE ACTUALLY MORE SPATIAL CONCEPT OF LANDING SITE.

- A landing site: any discerning that is to any degree locatable.
- All landing sites are marks or signals inscribed into the universe as the world.
- Body as mind sites itself as body. The same sets of landing sites, and no others, that define body define mind. Speak neither of mind nor body but of sets of landing sites.
- The sum of all landing sites equals a person or body plus world.
- The set of all landing sites of and for a person: ubiquitous site.
- Mould the ubiquitous (within a circumscribed area) site of a person as still another site. Duplicate the sets of landing sites that form a person or a community of persons.
- Ubiquitous sites within locally circumscribed areas have distinct foregrounds, middlegrounds, and backgrounds.

Briefly coordinated engagings of landing sites define (sculpt out) at least the following positions: forebackground, foreforeground, foremiddleground, middleforeground, middlemiddleground, middlebackground, backforeground, backmiddleground, backbackground, foreforeforeground, foreforemiddleground, foreforebackground; foremiddlebackground, foremiddleforeground, foremiddlemiddleground; forebackforeground, forebackmiddleground, forebackbackground; middleforeforeground, middleforemiddleground, middleforebackground; middlebackforeground, middlebackmiddleground, middlebackbackground; backforeforeground, backforemiddleground, backforebackground. Surprisingly, in the logical geographies of most philosophers, no note is made of these positionings as factors in the making of the world.

- We need neither painting nor sculpture but rather something to intervene between us and the world itself as painting or sculpture, the world as the work of art of the perceiver, or the world as architecture, an architecture of landing sites.
- Insert through Push enter Squeeze past Bend around Nearly filter by Split-land on the fly Zigzag tumble.
- It is in the nature of sensing or perceiving to land or be landing

Interpenetrating landing Upward landing Embracing landing Lateral landing Reluctant landing Penumbral landing Rising landing Subliminal landing Ricocheting landing.

- Involved in the composing of the world are three types of landing sites: perceptual, imaging, architectural. These may be different aspects or degrees of the same event.
- Landing sites should be thought of as sites on which to land and *sites that have landed or are landing*.
- All that is perceived is situated and therefore composed of landing sites.
- Landing sites never occur singly, only in sets.
- All perceptual points or areas of focus or all instances of perceptual attention are perceptual landing sites (visual, aural, tactile, olfactory, proprioceptive, kinaesthetic).
- The gaps between perceptual points or areas of focus are filled in by imaging landing sites. Imaging landing sites 'generalise' the world.
- Architectural landing sites determine form, dimension, and position.
- We chose not to decide yet on a particular scale for landing sites.
- Landing sites abound within landing sites.
- Any area that is neither a perceptual nor an architectural landing site is an imaging landing site.
- Construct the equivalent of those sets of landing sites necessary and sufficient to the constituting of a body.
- Associate every material with a particular sound. Six or seven distinctly different orders should be placed within a twenty-foot square.
- These constructions will be tentative constructed plans in respect to which a person will know herself as site. Eventually these constructions may be capable of forming a perceiver from scratch. It is useful to think in terms of both goals – perceiving in relation to such a plan and generating a new perceiver – at once. We suspect that once we sketch in the outlines, certain processes in the universe will 'know' how to join in and do their share. Our role in this is to cause radical reconfigurations of landing sites.
- Each person constructs an impalpable and indiscernible tentative plan in respect to her surroundings. We will build our discernible constructed plans to be tentative: they will, until they become definitive, always be subject to change.
- The fielding of the world equals ubiquitous site. Tentative constructed plans continually, everywhere they sit, and in all their angles, situate and define ubiquitous site.

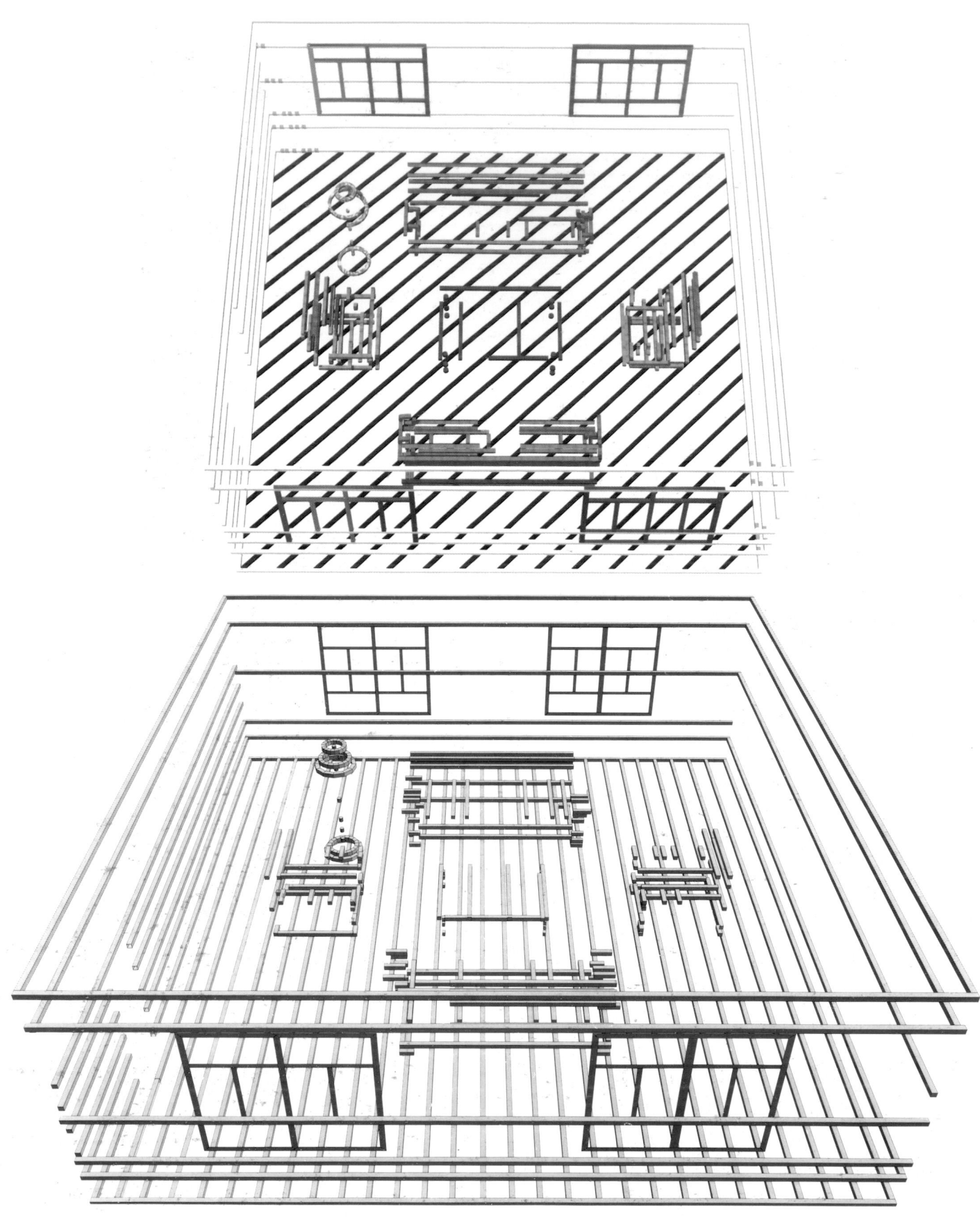

Any form can be thought of as a set of guiding or engaging bars

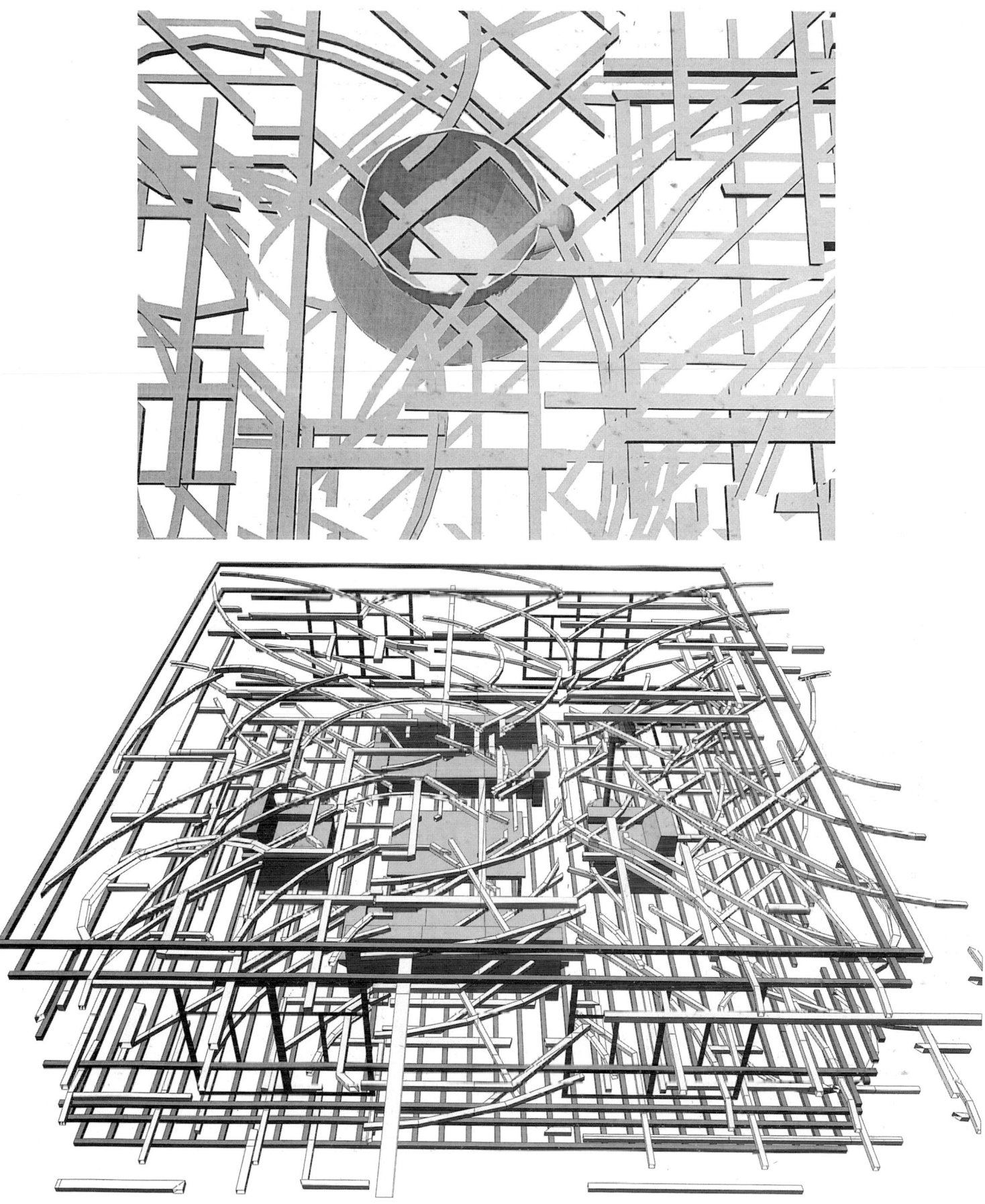

Just as a guiding bar might be placed wherever a perceptual landing site has occurred, wherever a guiding or engaging bar has been placed, a perceptual landing site might occur

Surrounding an object with guiding or engaging bars adds more perceptual landing sites to the sequence of landing sites by which it is perceived or put to use

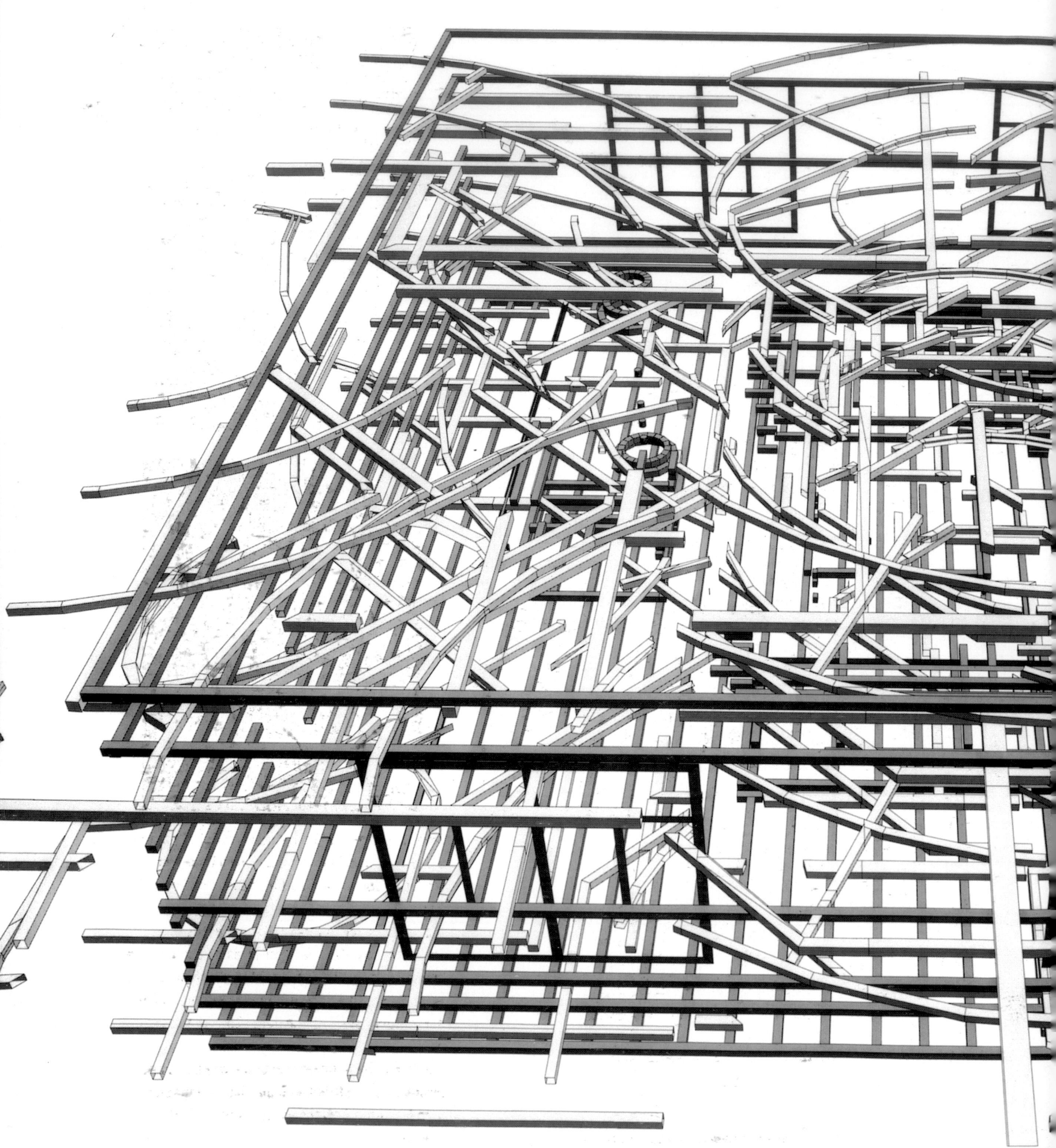

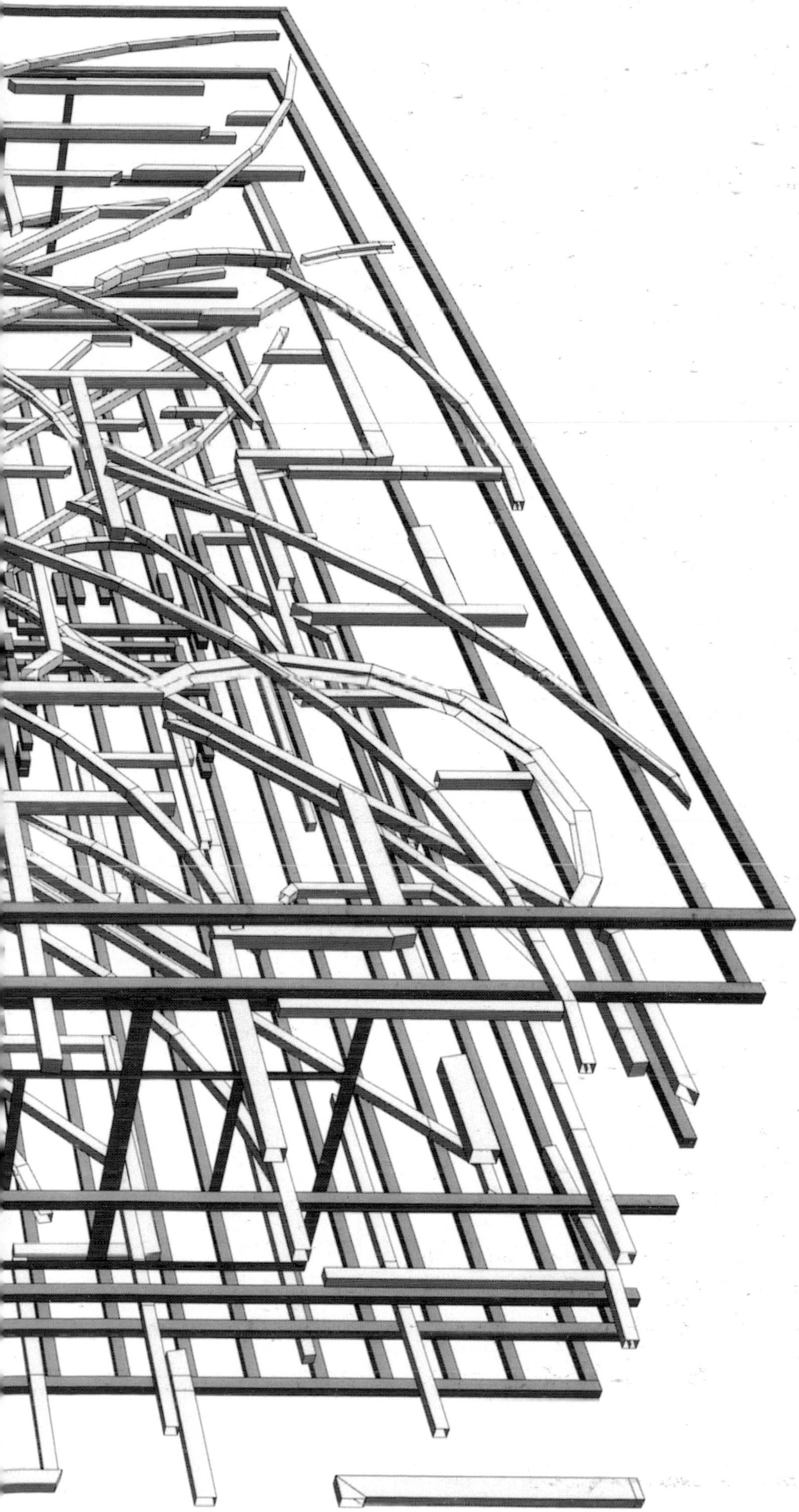

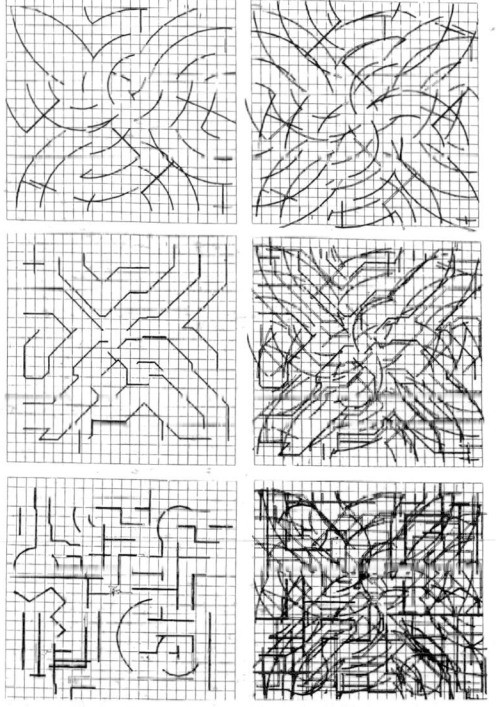

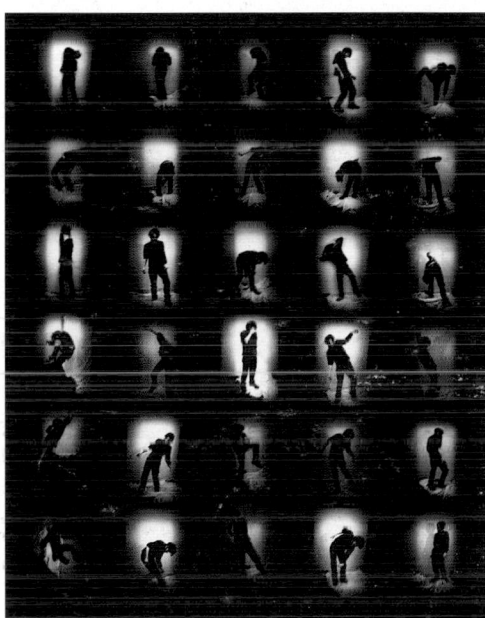

Guiding or engaging bars characterise, by means of their form and placement, how a body has moved or could move. What is the site of a person?

In the end, each of three labyrinth patterns repeats twice. Each twin reverses its double, and one of each pair is 15 per cent larger than the other. This is but one solution to the problem of how guiding or engaging bars should be positioned

The forms the body must assume when passing through a room filled with guiding or engaging bars influence how the world forms, how it appears

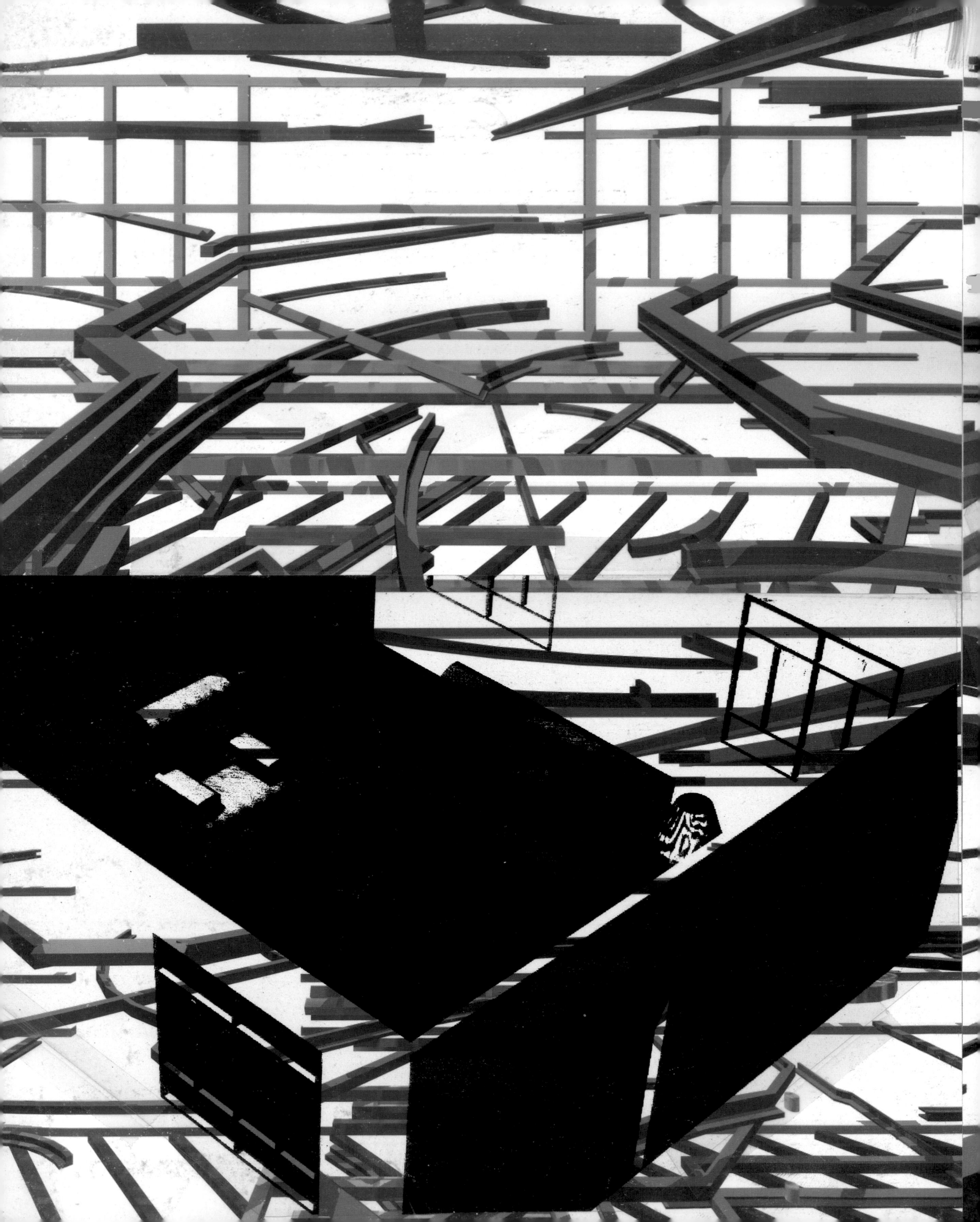

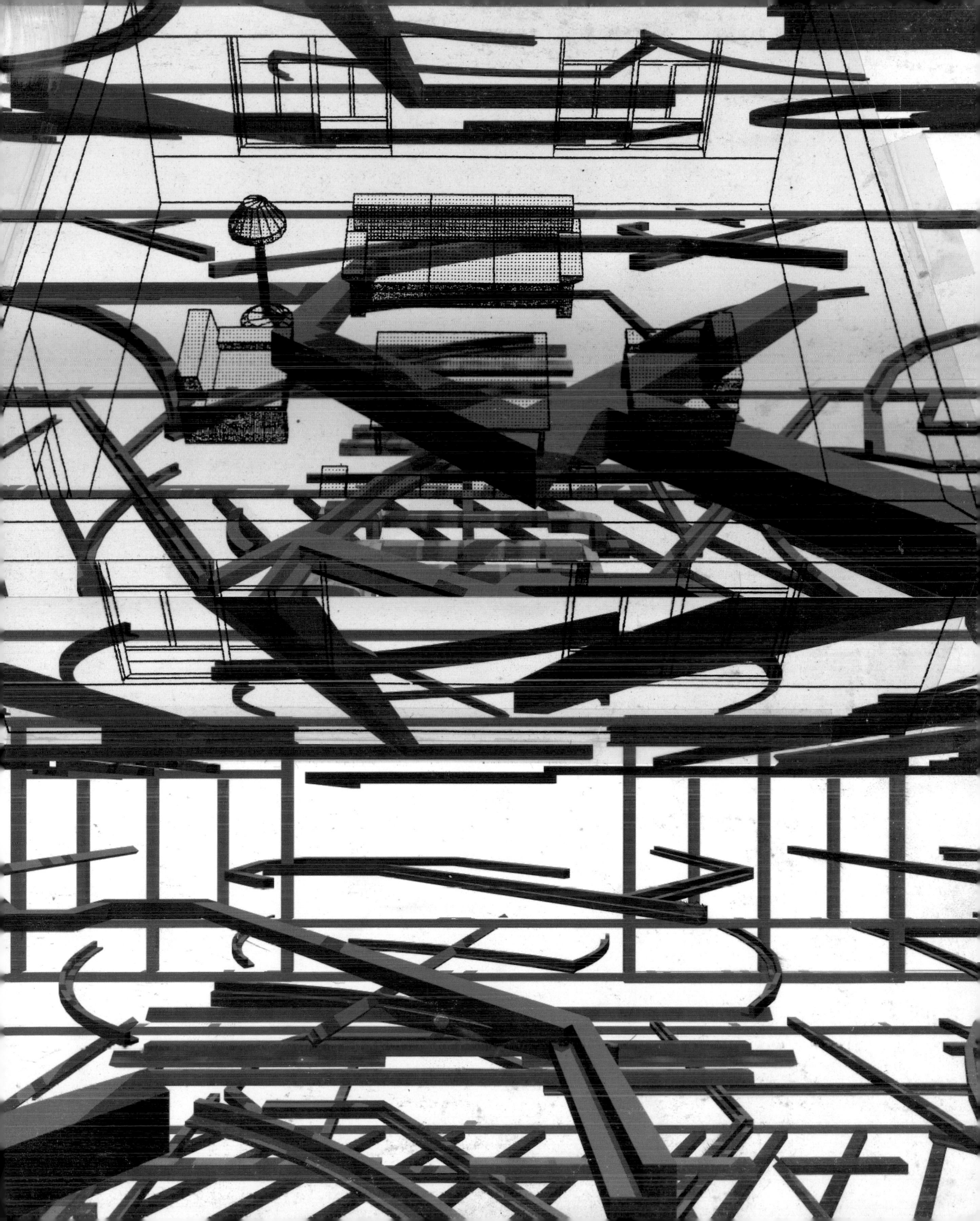

Standing in the middle of a room filled with
guiding or engaging bars and looking from wall to
wall, the observer will exhibit less than the usual
tendency to form objects

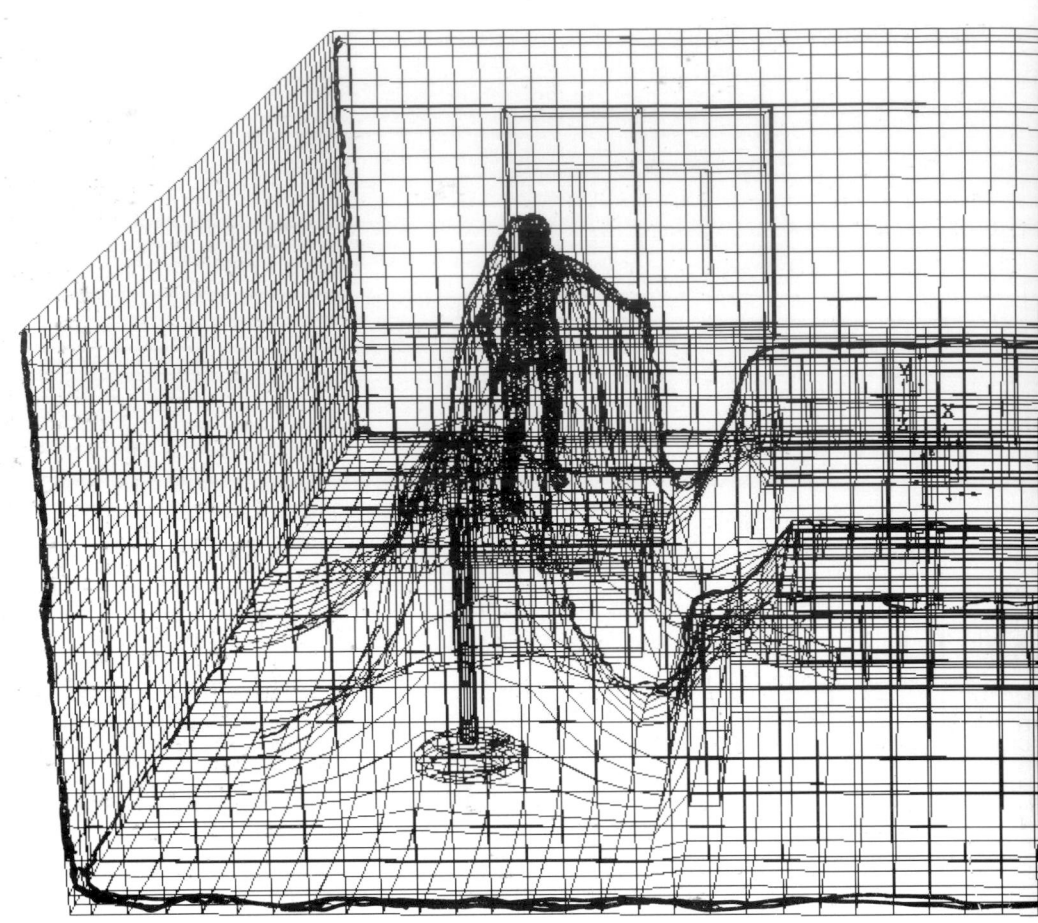

Landing sites shift and the appearance of the
world changes according to how the body moves

An engaging envelope replaces the engaging
bars, surrounds the ubiquitous site and fills it as
if it were a mould

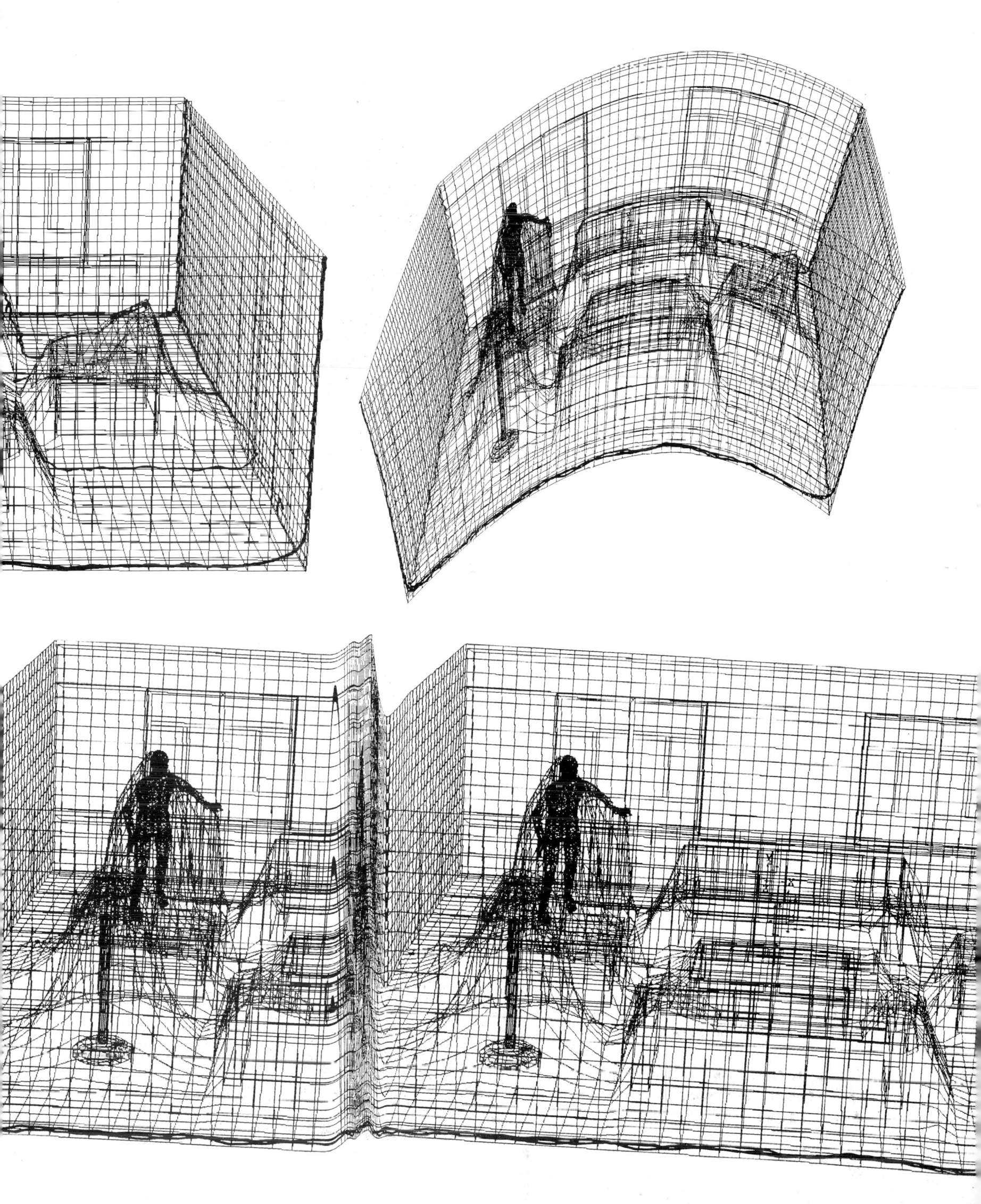

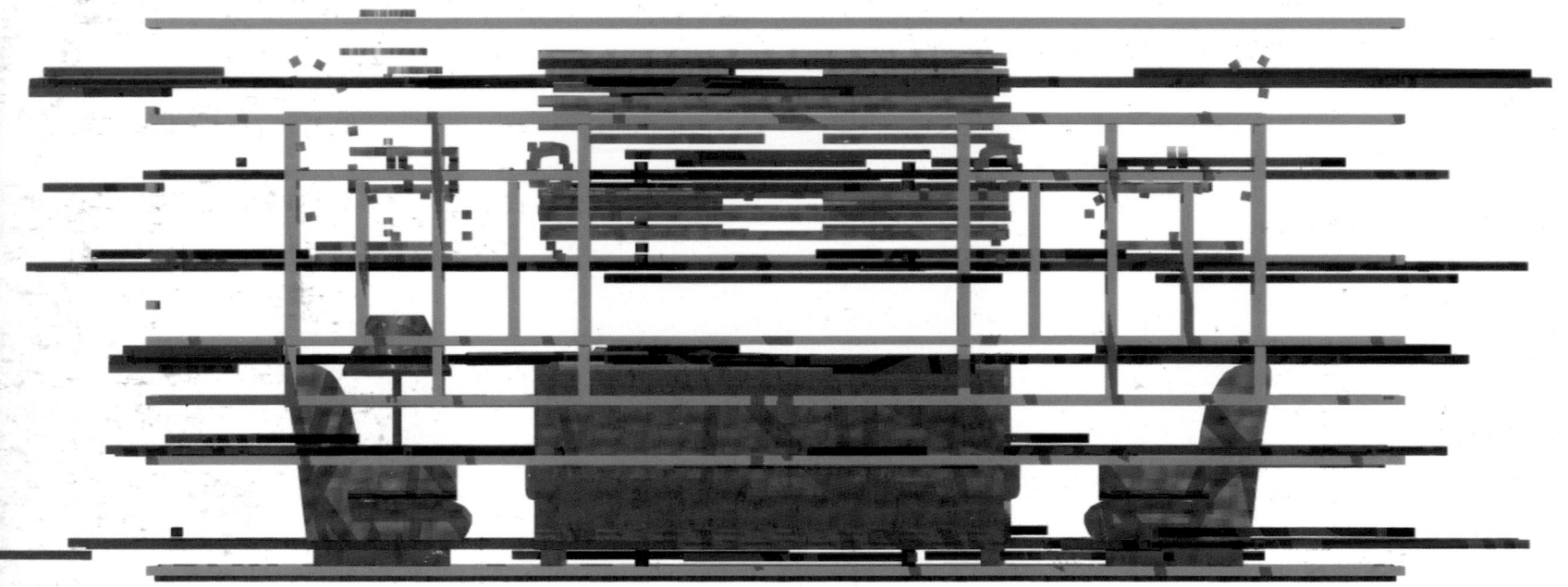

Doubling the furniture puts a new floor level or a plateau in place without one actually having to be built

Two representative stages in the perceiving of the same set of objects are juxtaposed. Each set (a different stage in the perceiving) serves as the ostensive definition of the other or of 'the processing of the other'

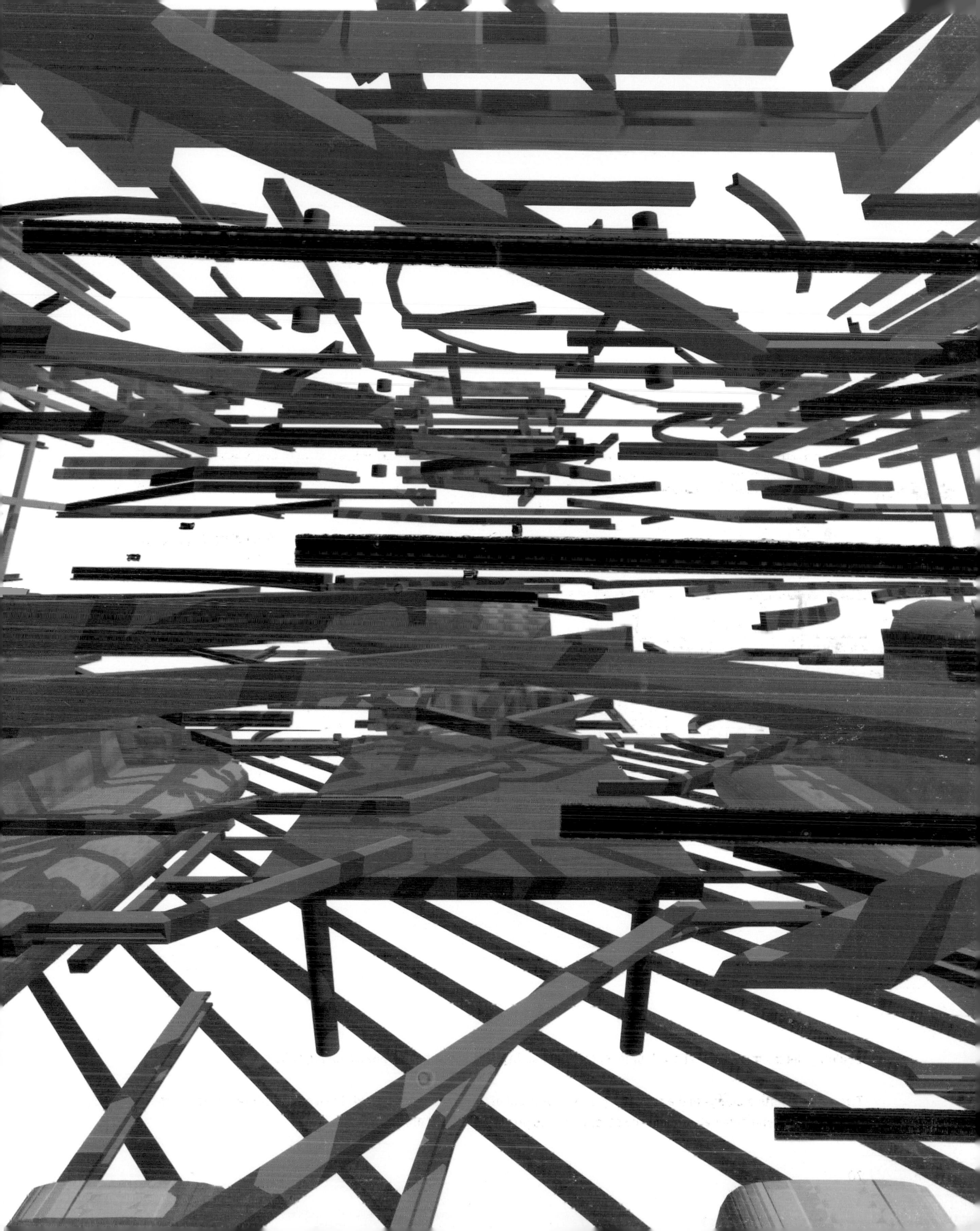

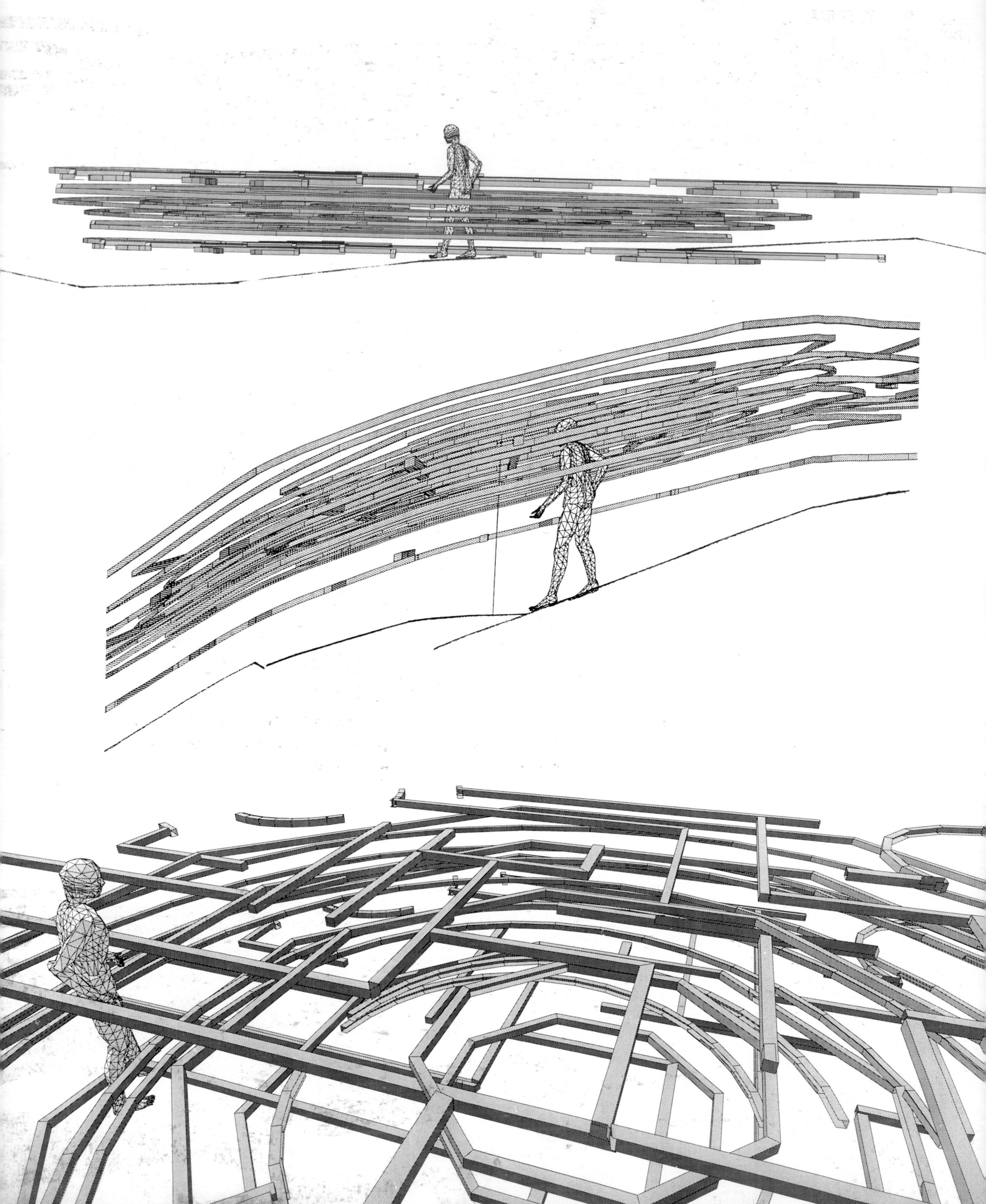

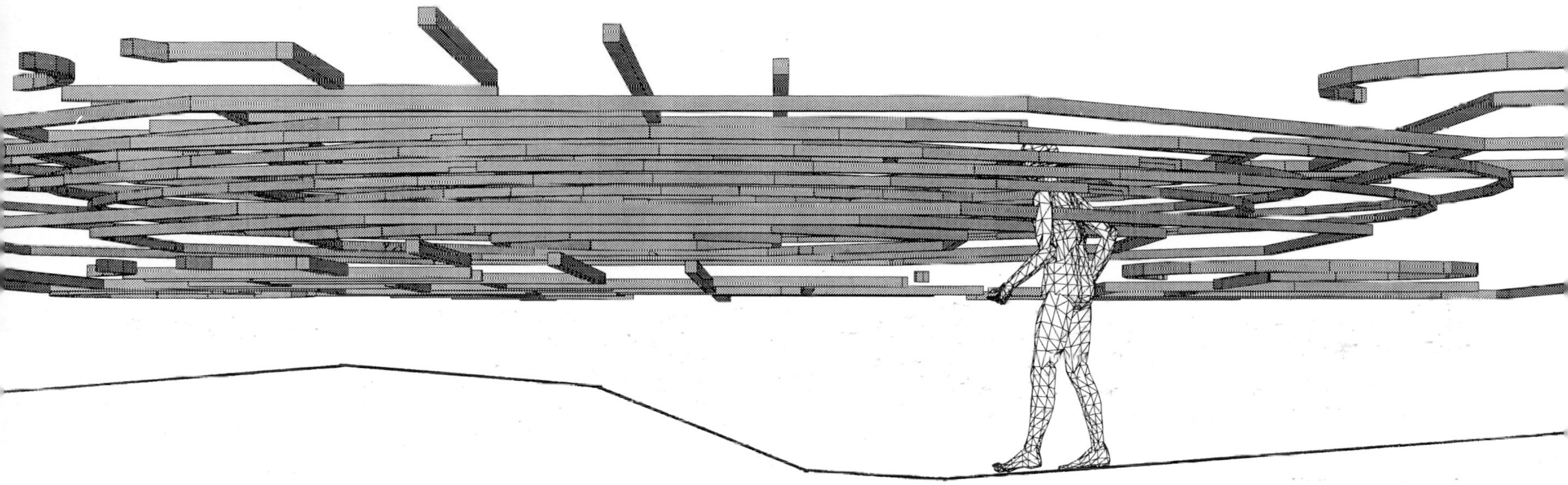

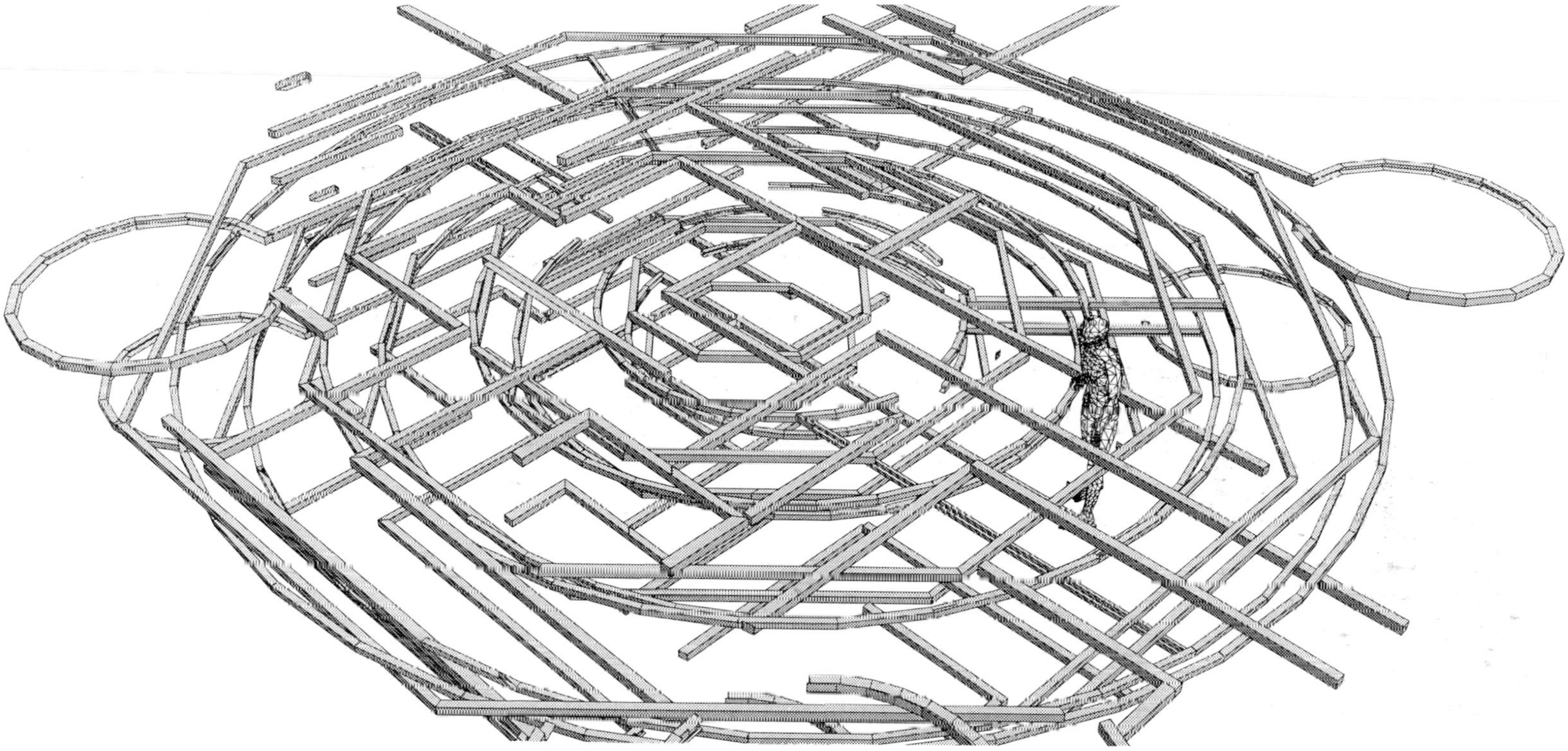

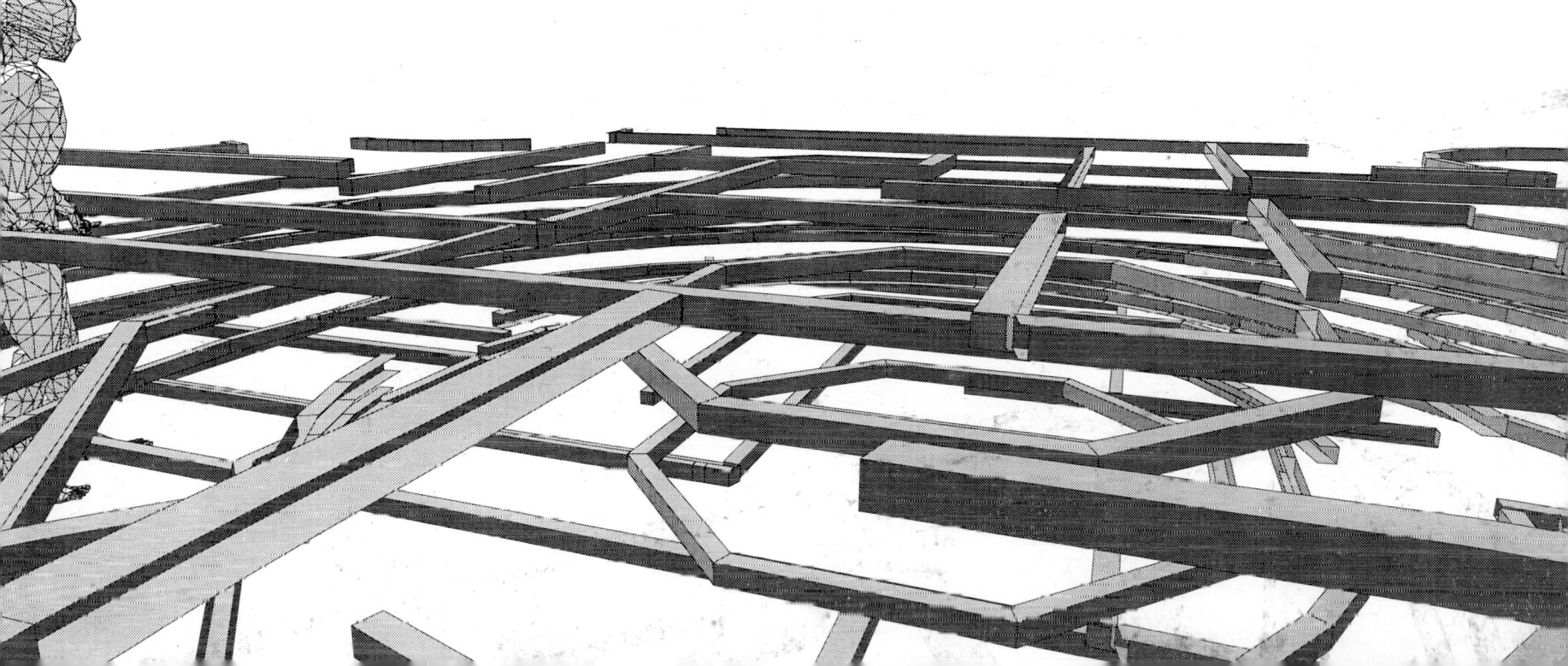

Distinctly different labyrinths are positioned one above the other so as to remain simultaneously viewable. Movements elicited by the guiding or engaging bars of one labyrinth level often contradict movements suggested by guiding or engaging bars directly above or below. Although it is desirable to avoid constructing labyrinths with centres, this is not always possible

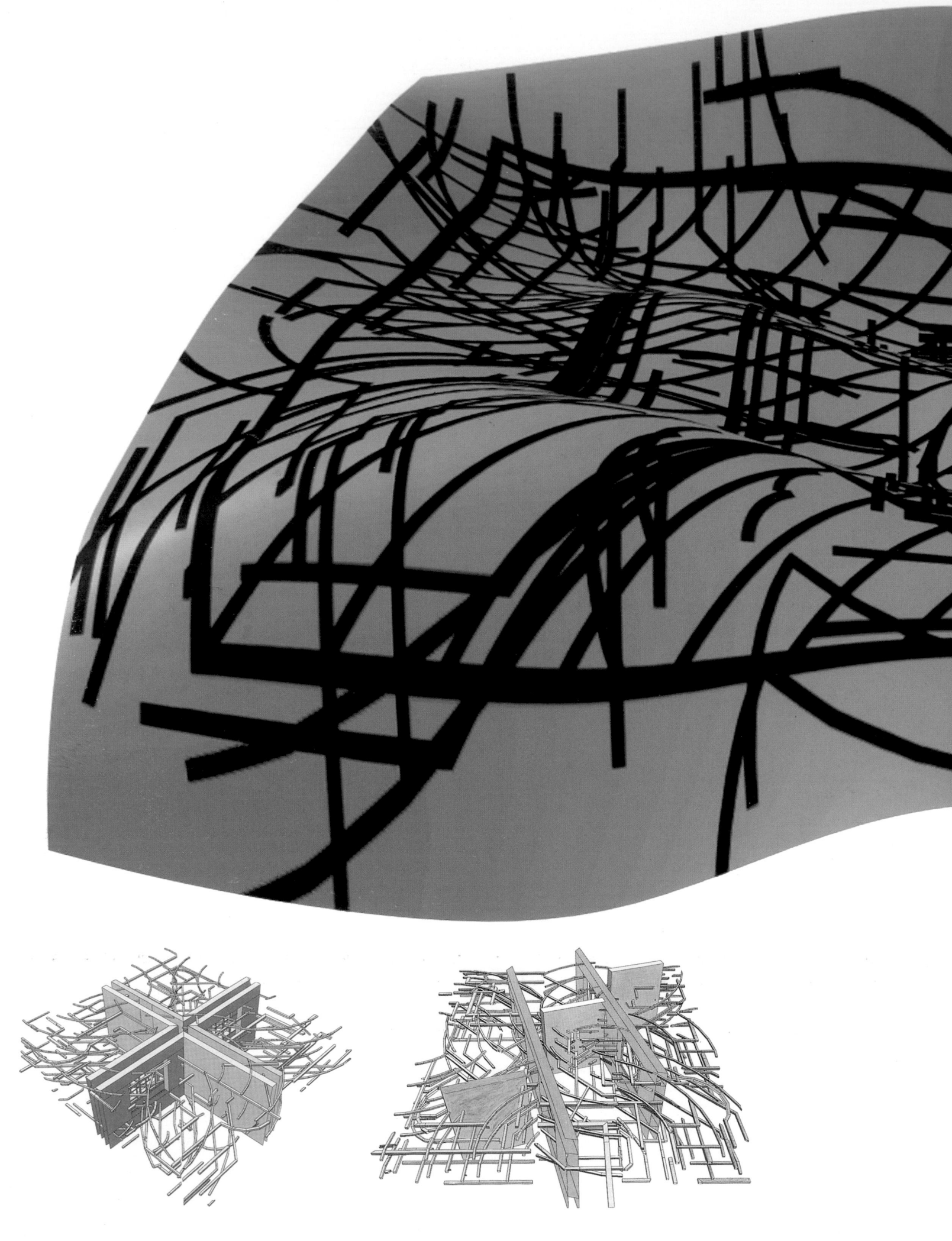

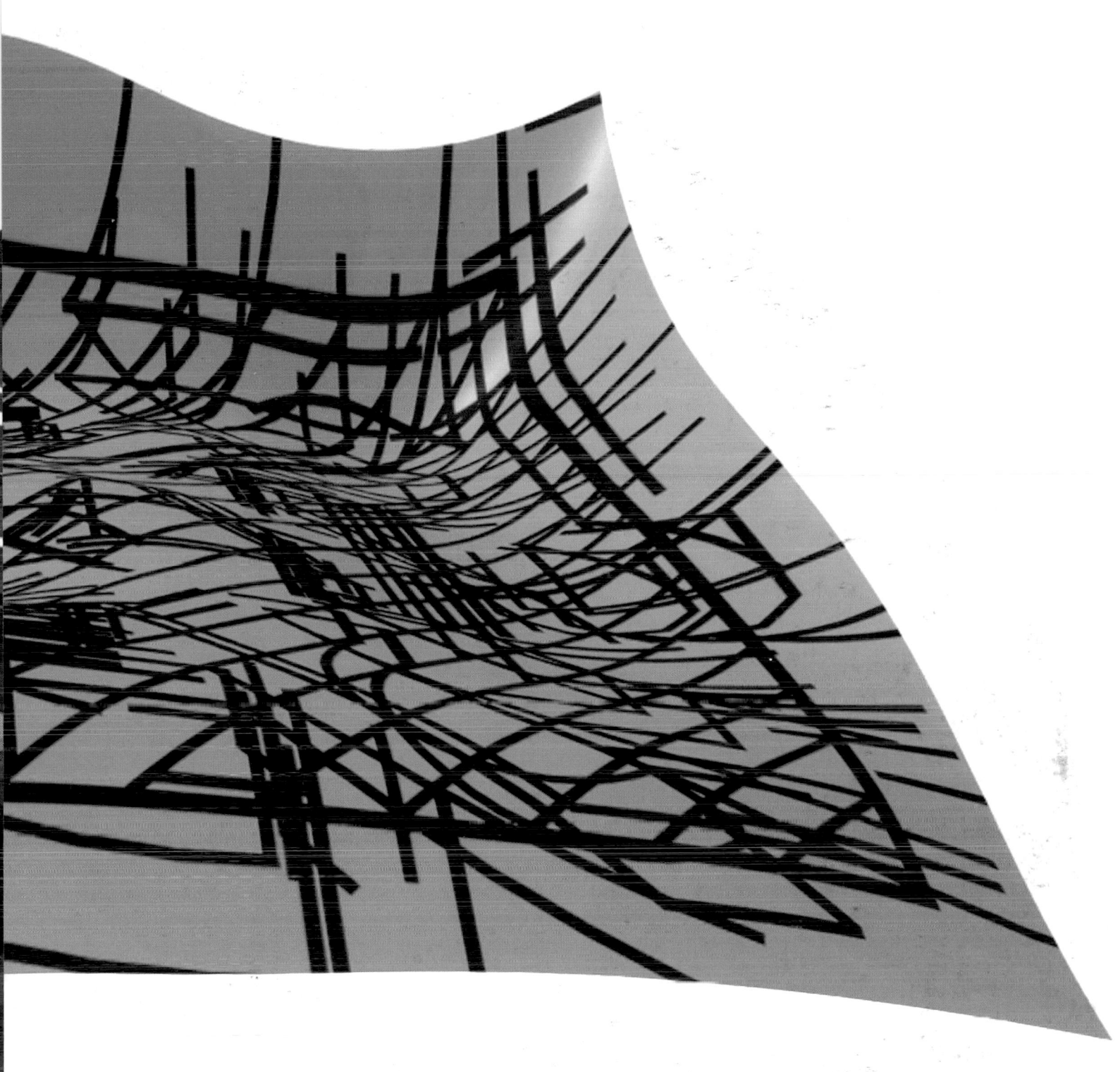

To maximise combinatorial possibilities for landing sites, all floors should become terrains. Every square foot must be treated differently. Attention to the complexity of terrains is fundamental to the ecology of landing sites.

Anything that will set fewer arbitrary limits on landing sites should be tried

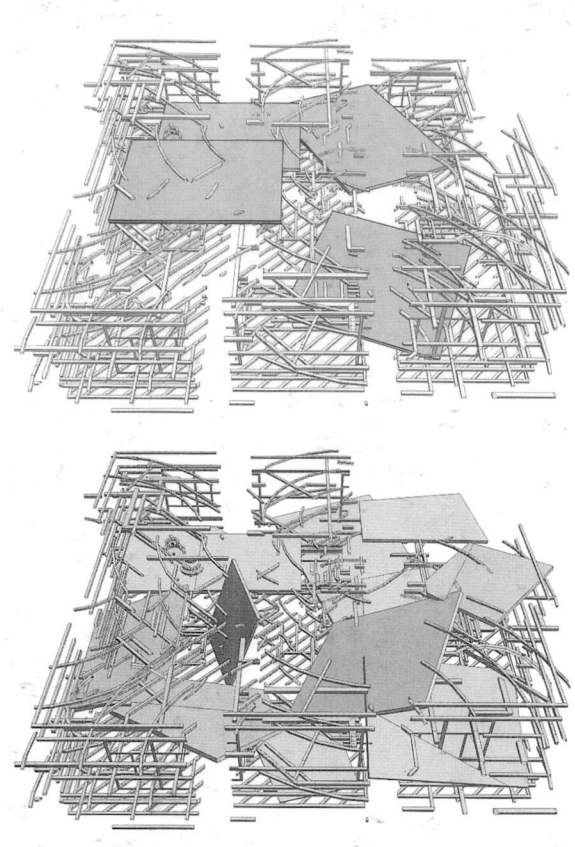

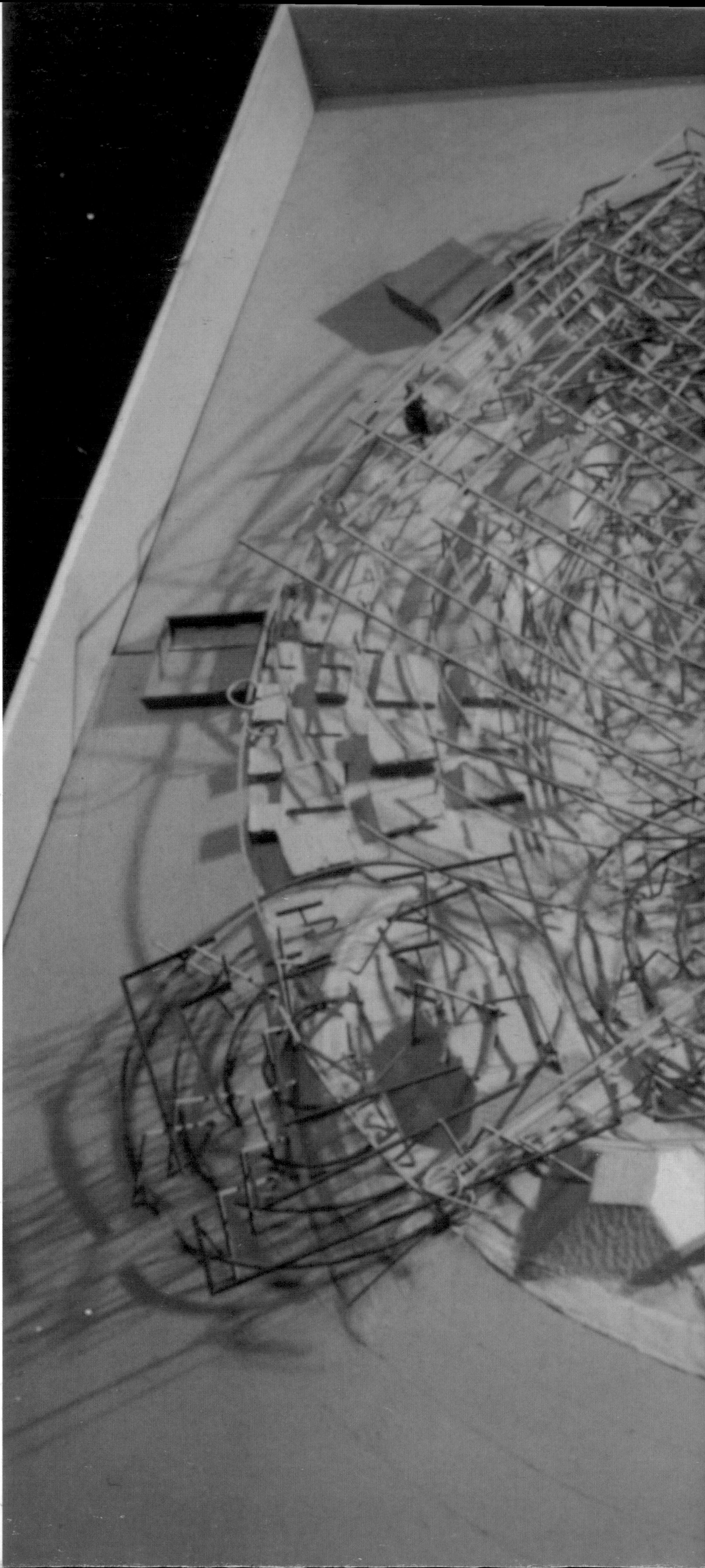

Even those plateaus that are out of the body's reach and are accessible only to perception invite action. Horizontal and vertical plateaus, and everything between

Site of Reversible Destiny (for a community of landing sites): model of a three-hundred-square-foot construction on which work is scheduled to begin in 1994

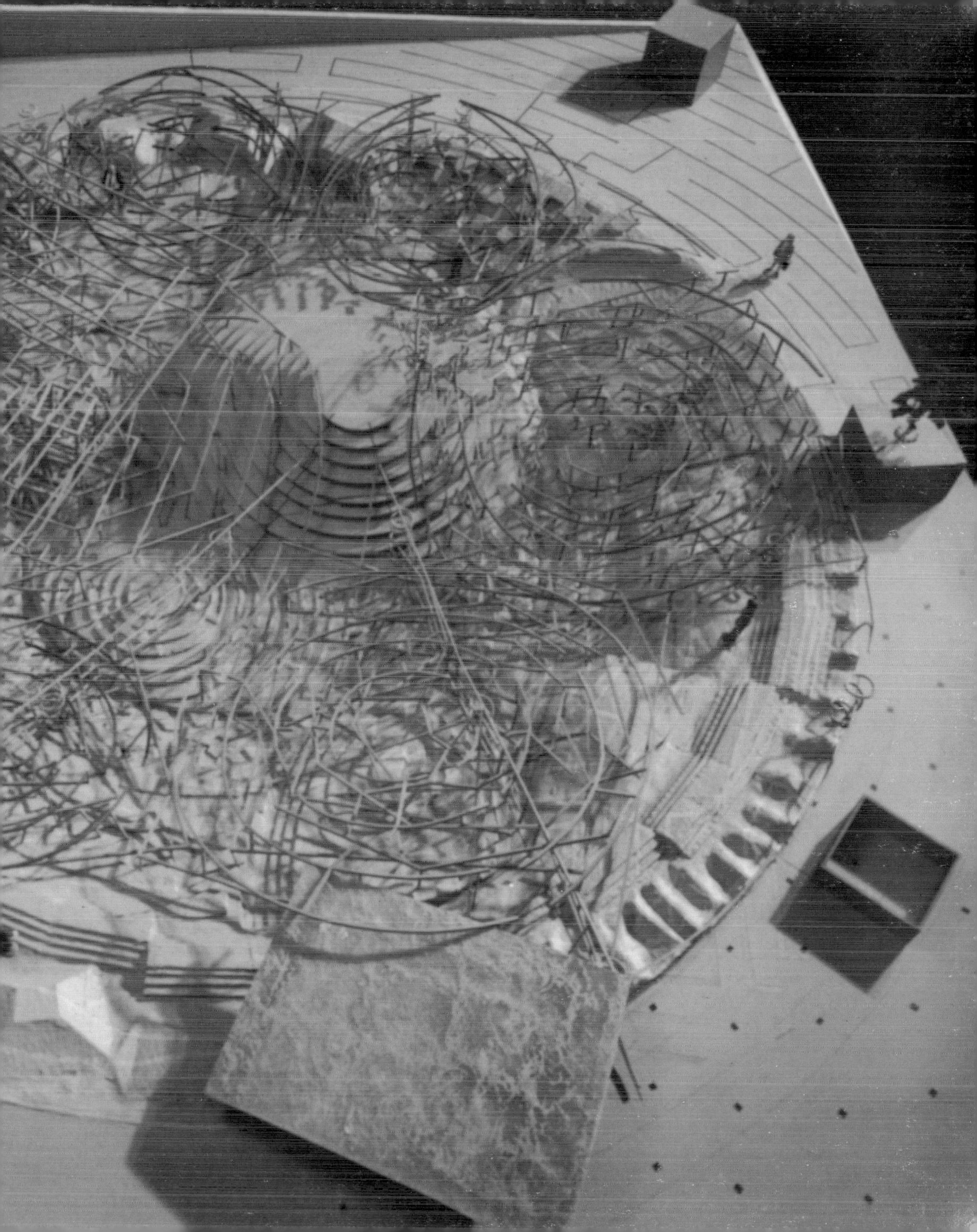

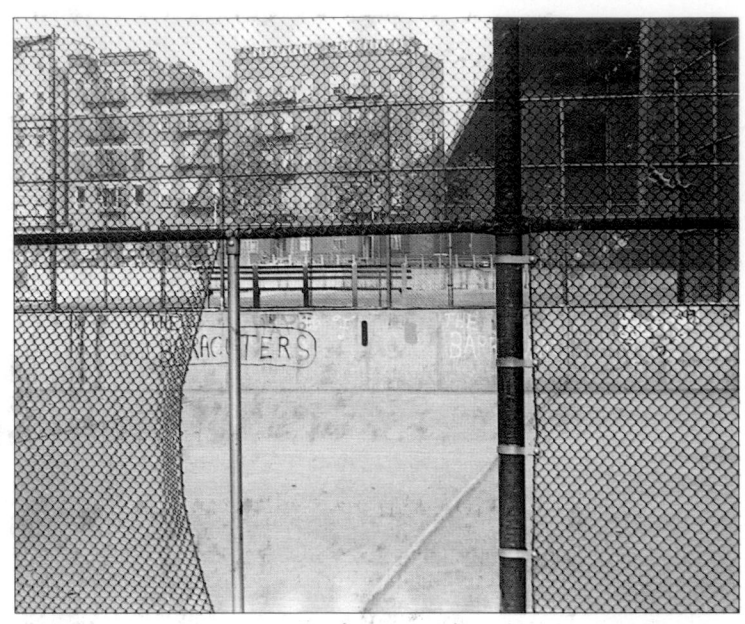
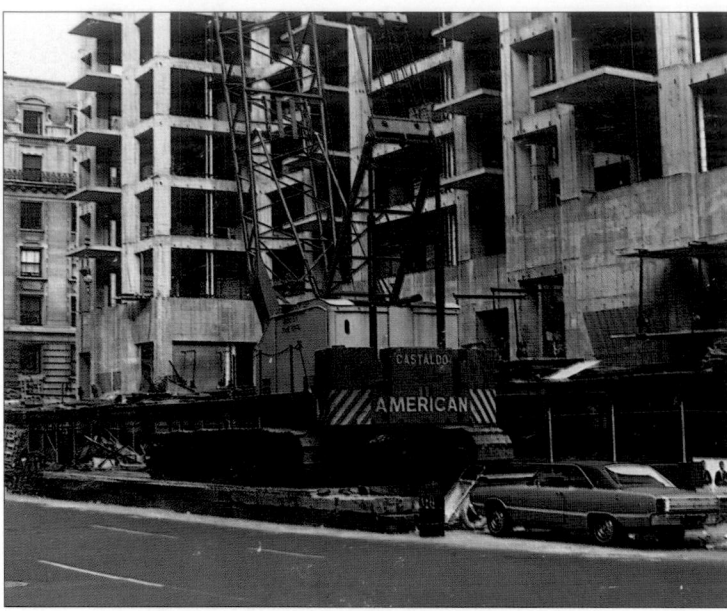
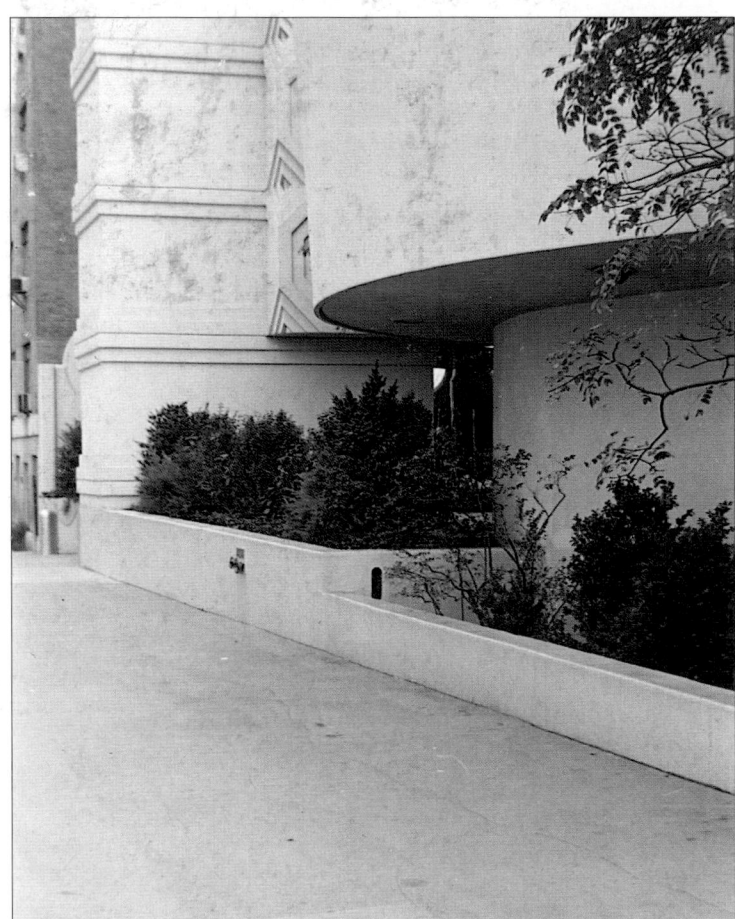
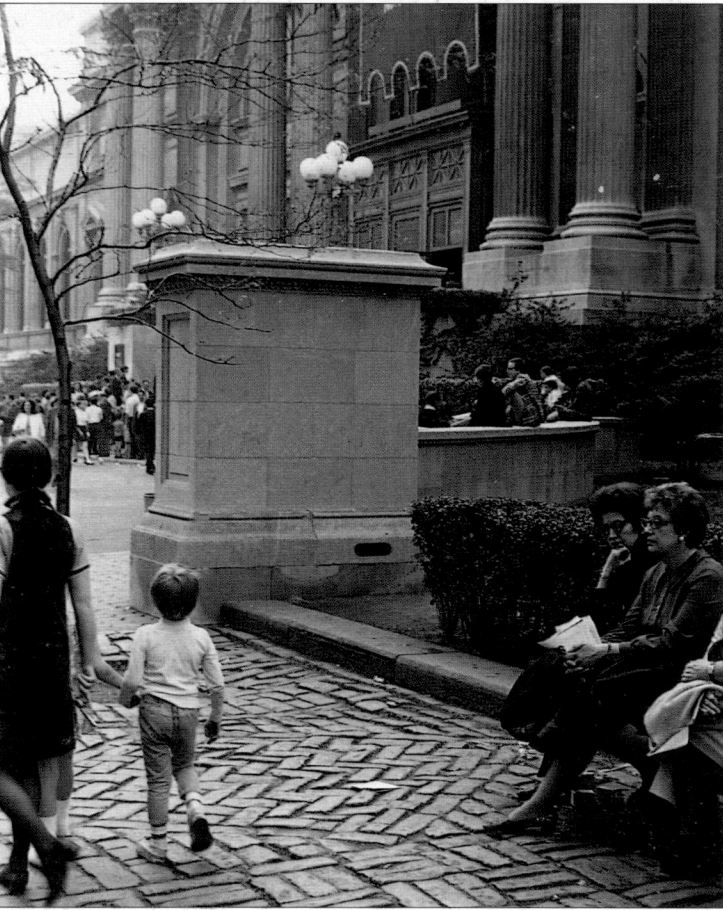

RICHARD ARTSCHWAGER

Art and design operate in the same territory, however different they may be from each other. And they are different, the latter being given to the useful and the former to the useless. It always comes down to that; in fine that distinction makes the terms useful to us.

Since both operate in the same physical territory, a considerable mixing of the two is to be expected, no?! The notion 'Installation' addressed this state of affairs directly, and I think the two works of mine herein presented, might shed some light, or at least give an idea of the range that is possible.

First the *blp*. It is a mindless invasion of the social space by a logo-like, totally useless art element. It is small, has high visibility, relentlessly refuses to give up its uselessness. It is an instrument for useless looking. Being of small size and high visibility it converts the immediate surround over to The Useless. That is its 'function'. It gets as close to pure art as one can get.

Now, for *Generations*. It is an insertion, like the *blp*, but differs in that it is at one with the scale of the natural and cultural paraphernalia around it, mimics the various elements of this paraphernalia, and in other ways insinuates itself into the context. It leaves intact, at best celebrates, the existing use/purpose of the ground which it has pre-empted. More directly, it gives itself to the pre-existent use of this ground which is itself part of the larger social (ie, useful) space.

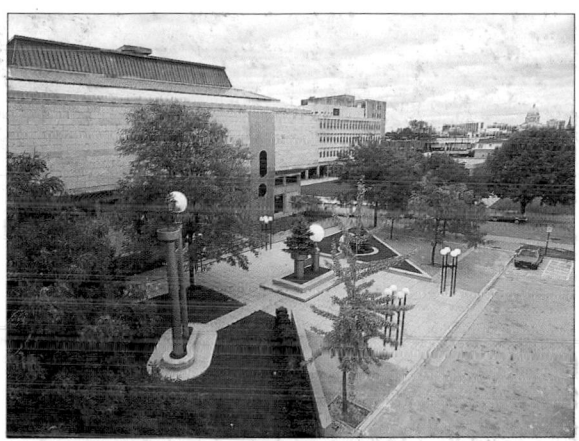

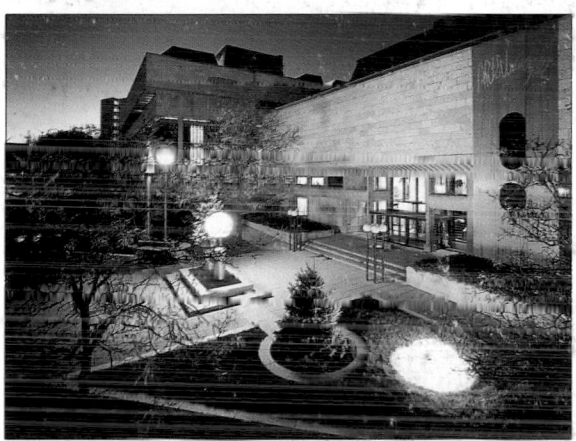

ABOVE AND BELOW: Generations, 1990-91, Elvehjem Museum of Art, Madison, Wisconsin; OPPOSITE, ABOVE LEFT: blp, c1971, New York; ABOVE RIGHT: blp, c1971, New York; BELOW LEFT: blp, c1971, installed outside the Solomon R Guggenheim Museum, New York; BELOW RIGHT: blp, c1971, installed outside the Metropolitan Museum of Art, New York

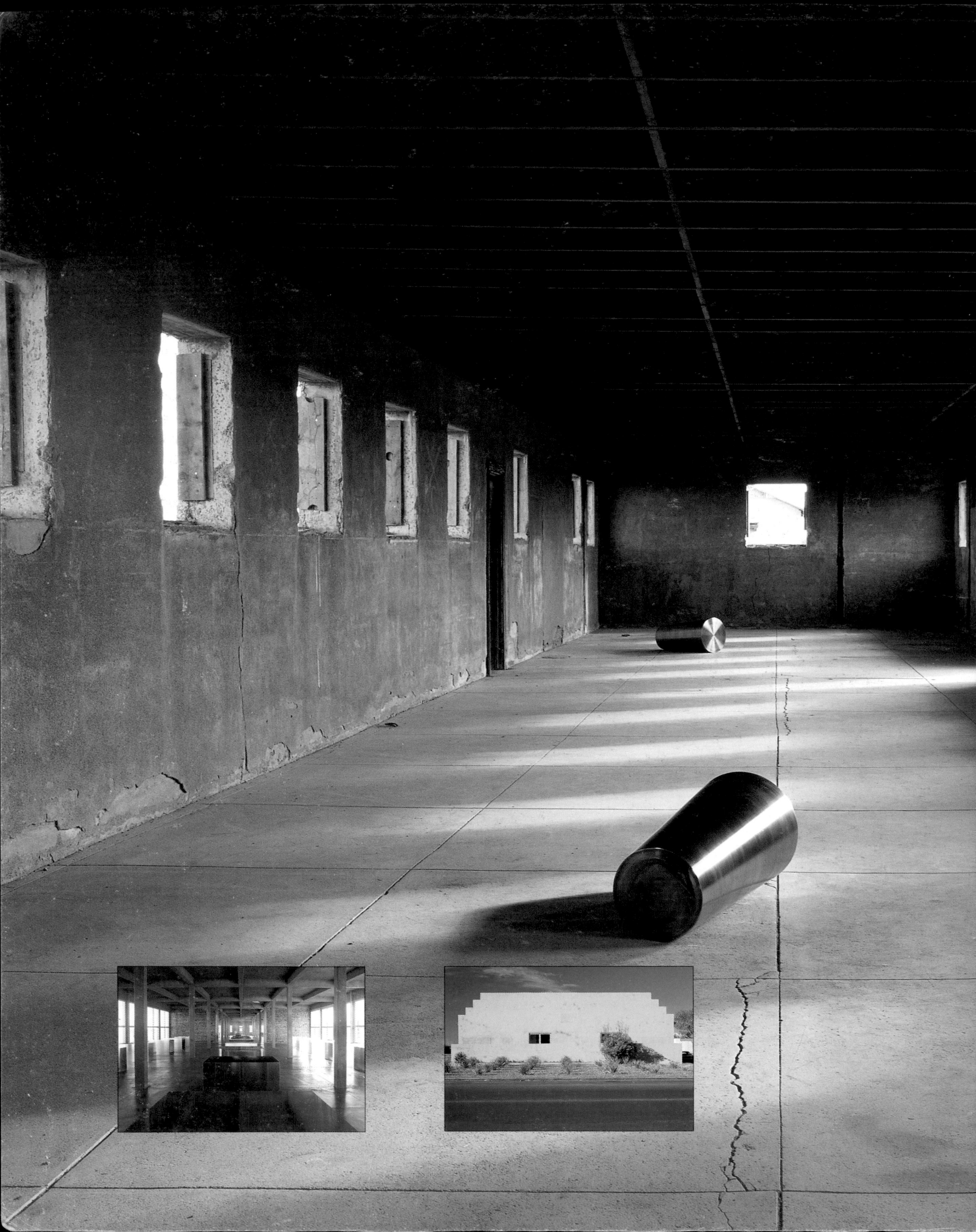

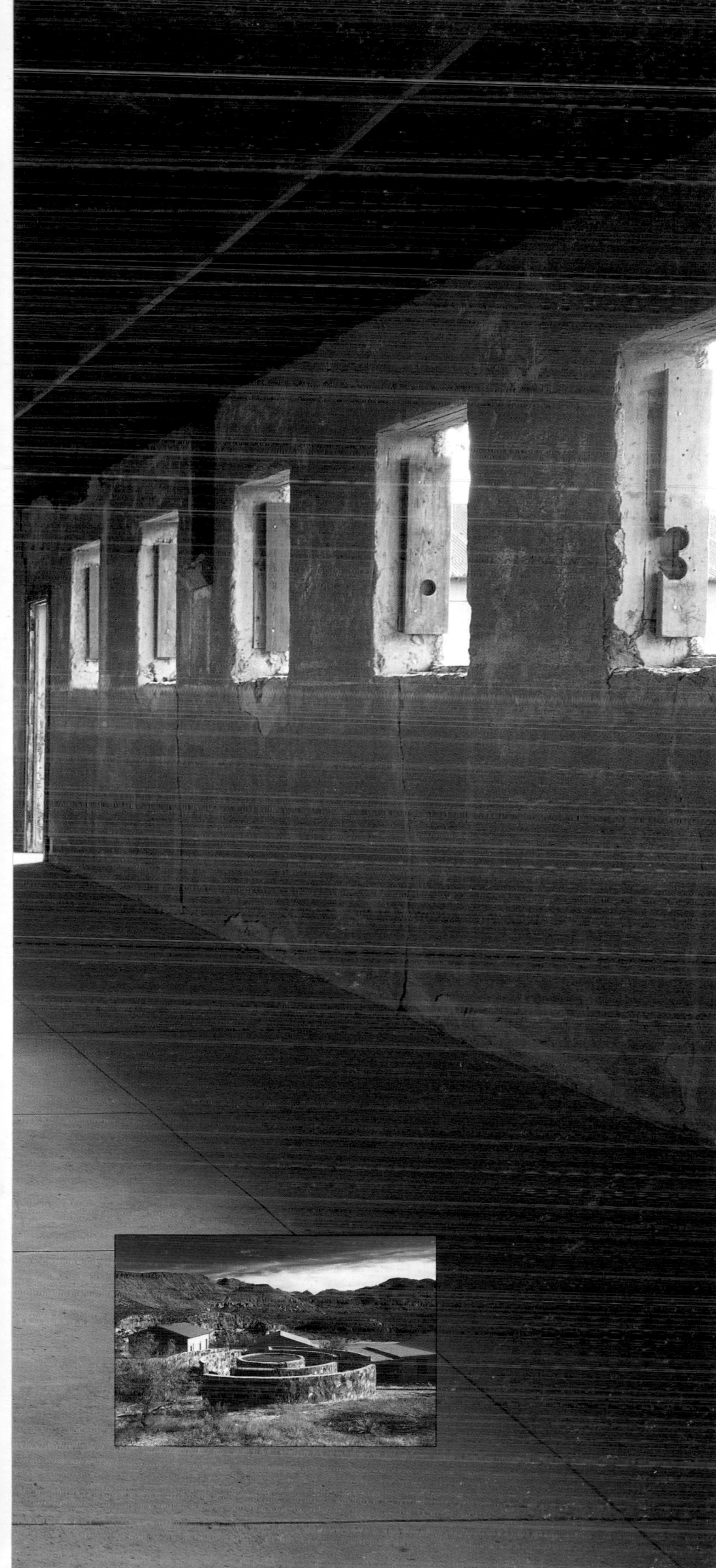

DONALD JUDD

A good installation is too much work and too expensive and if the artist does it, too personal, to then destroy. Paintings, sculptures and other three-dimensional work cannot withstand the constant installation and removal and shipping. The perpetual show business is beyond the museum's finances and capacities. The show business museum gets built but the art does not, nor even handled well, when the art is the reason for the building. And the architecture is well below and behind the best art. An example of something much better for less money is to have saved Les Halles in Paris, an important deed itself, and then to have given two hundred thousand dollars each, sufficient at the time, to a dozen of the world's best artists to make work to remain forever. This would have been the achievement of the century. Instead Beaubourg was built, an expensive, disproportionate monster, romanticising the machinery of an oil refinery, not scarce. The building makes change the main characteristic of paintings and sculptures that don't change. The building and the change are just show business, visual comedy.

Donald Judd's work and work by other artists is permanently installed at the Chinati Foundation, Marfa, Texas; MAIN PICTURE: *Roni Horn,* For a Here and a There; LEFT: *Artillery Shed interior, with works by Donald Judd, permanent installation;* CENTRE: *Chamberlain Building (exterior);* RIGHT: *Overview, Ayala de Chinati Ranch, Presidio County, Texas (photos: Todd Eberle)*

ANYA GALLACCIO

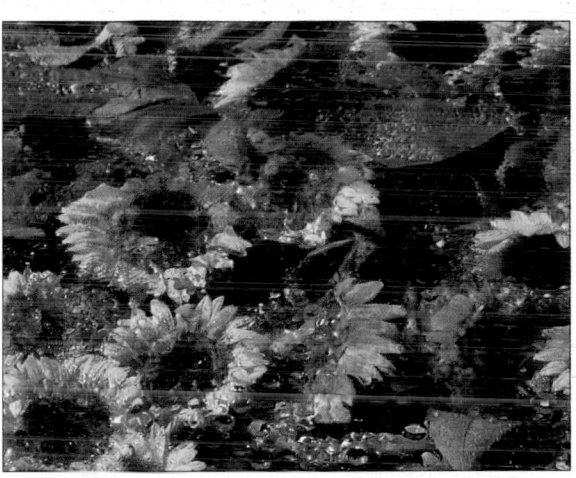

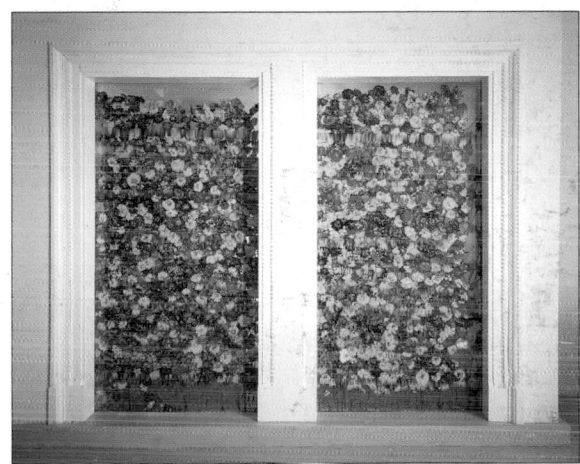

I wanted to create a red room. The colour is as important as the fact that they are roses. The piece will have an initial glowing vibrancy, but then the petals will turn brown, like scabs, wound-like dried scabs. The thorns and stems, which will be underneath the petals, could be seen as a reminder of something quite dangerous. I like the mixture of celebration with death or decay – but it is important that people bring their own experience to the work, it is evocative and sensual enough to enable this to happen. The previous works I made using Sunflowers and the Gerberas became unintentionally destructive. By putting a sheet of glass on them, and attempting to preserve and present the flowers, the condensation which they produced actually led to them decaying even faster, it speeded up the process which made something else happen. The piece at the ICA has similar concerns but it won't be as dramatic. I am trying to make this piece last and let the roses die out so that I can do something else with them.

I see my works as being a performance and a collaboration. It adds something to the work that isn't obvious. With the piece where I used a ton of oranges I had to individually remove each label. When I initially threw them on the warehouse floor, where they were sited, they got dirty so they had to be polished and carefully placed. It took about three days. To me these hidden, ritualistic activities are important. The attention to detail and care is maybe another feminine aspect, but I don't want the labour to be obvious. Where the obsessive quality is too blatant it obscures the joy of simply experiencing the piece in a more celebratory way. it is like the hidden domestic activities of how many times you cook dinner and how many times you clean the bath, but I don't want it to become a chore. The magic and the pleasure have to be the most important things.

ABOVE: Preserve Sunflower, 1991, detail, 101 sunflowers; BELOW: Untitled, 1992, 1,600 zinnias; OPPOSITE: Red on Green, 1992, ICA, London (photo: Edward Woodman)

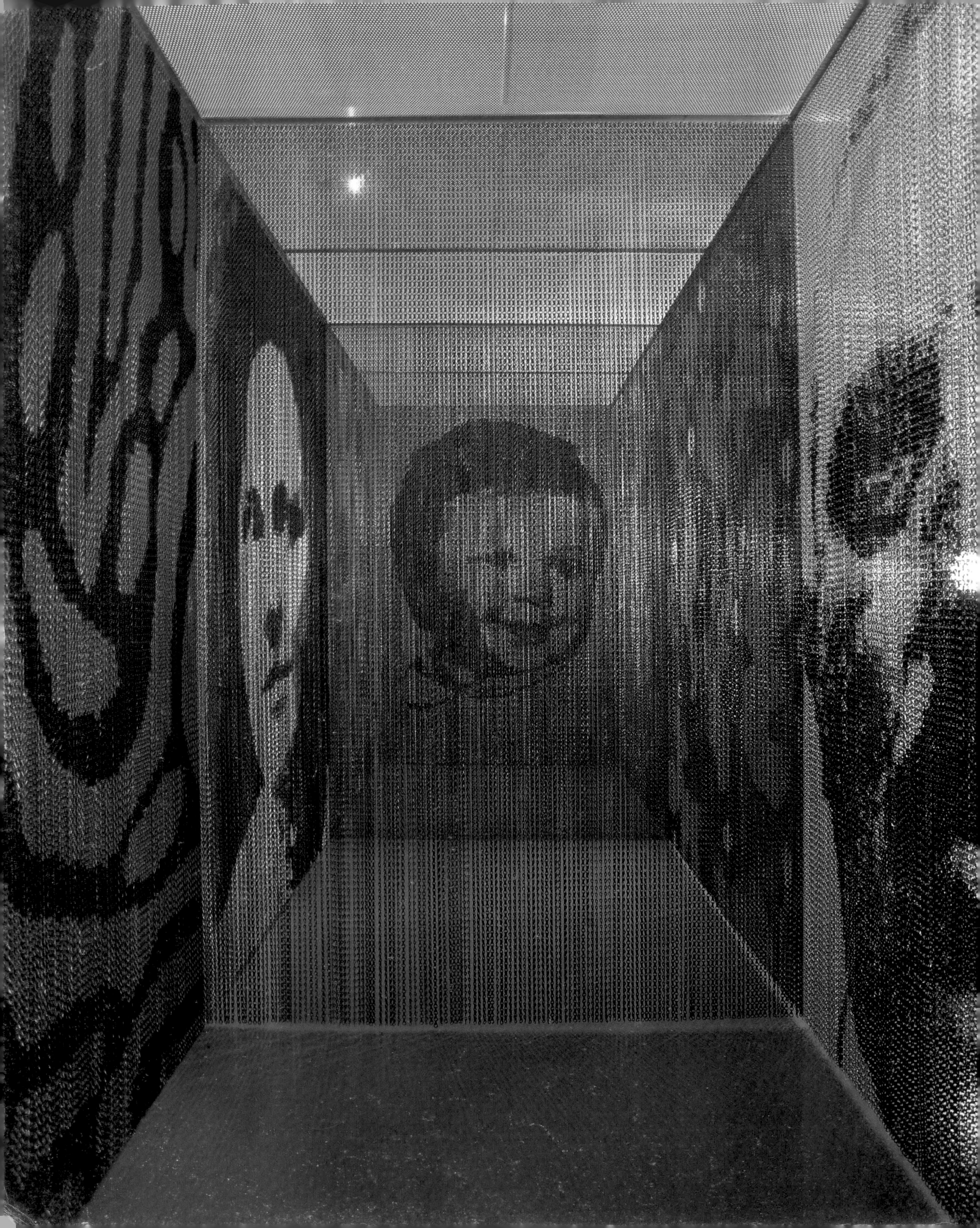

ANDREW SABIN
THE SEA OF SUN

Installation is an aspect of sculpture as is its antithesis, the object. Their relationship is similar to that between notions of subjectivity and objectivity. With installation the viewer is always implicated in the work whilst with objects they are separate. As with their psychological equivalent absolute objects and total installations are unstable entities, their relationship being so intimate that the one reverts to the other at the flicker of a doubting thought.

In theory the parts of an object are in particular relation to each other whilst the context of the whole is a moveable feast that affects none of the implications of the work. In installation the viewer becomes the object that observes its context. The sculptural arena can therefore be seen as an infinite number of centres surveying a circumference or towards a circumference scrutinising its centre.

At BAC, *The Sea of Sun* occupied the entire volume of the gallery. To enter the gallery was to enter the work. Once inside the viewers found themselves in an environment divided by veils of physically and visually permeable surfaces. As the viewers move from enclosure to enclosure they animate the work both optically, by changing the relationship between units of information on each successive veil, and physically by creating a wake as they push their way through the space.

The Sea of Sun will be shown again as an installation at the Henry Moore Institute in November, 1993. If a large enough venue or suitable outdoor site is found, *The Sea of Sun* will be shown as an object to be approached from afar and entered at any point around its boundary. It goes without saying that once entered the object reverts to installation.

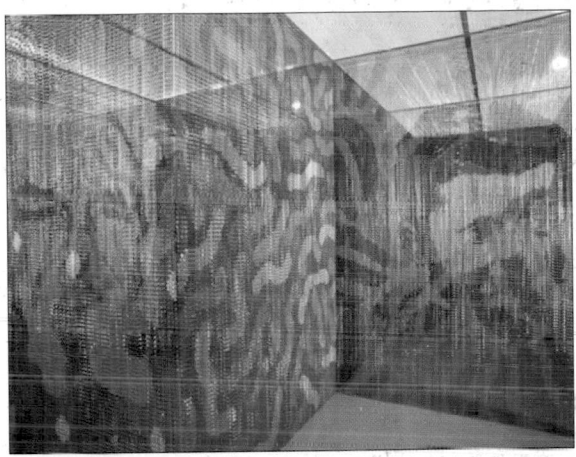

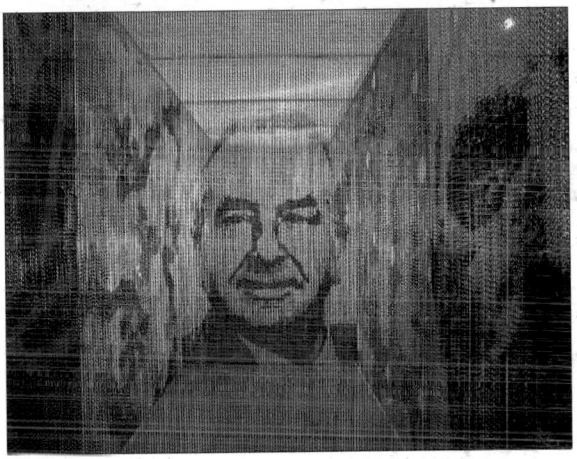

The Sea of Sun, *1992, Battersea Arts Centre, London*

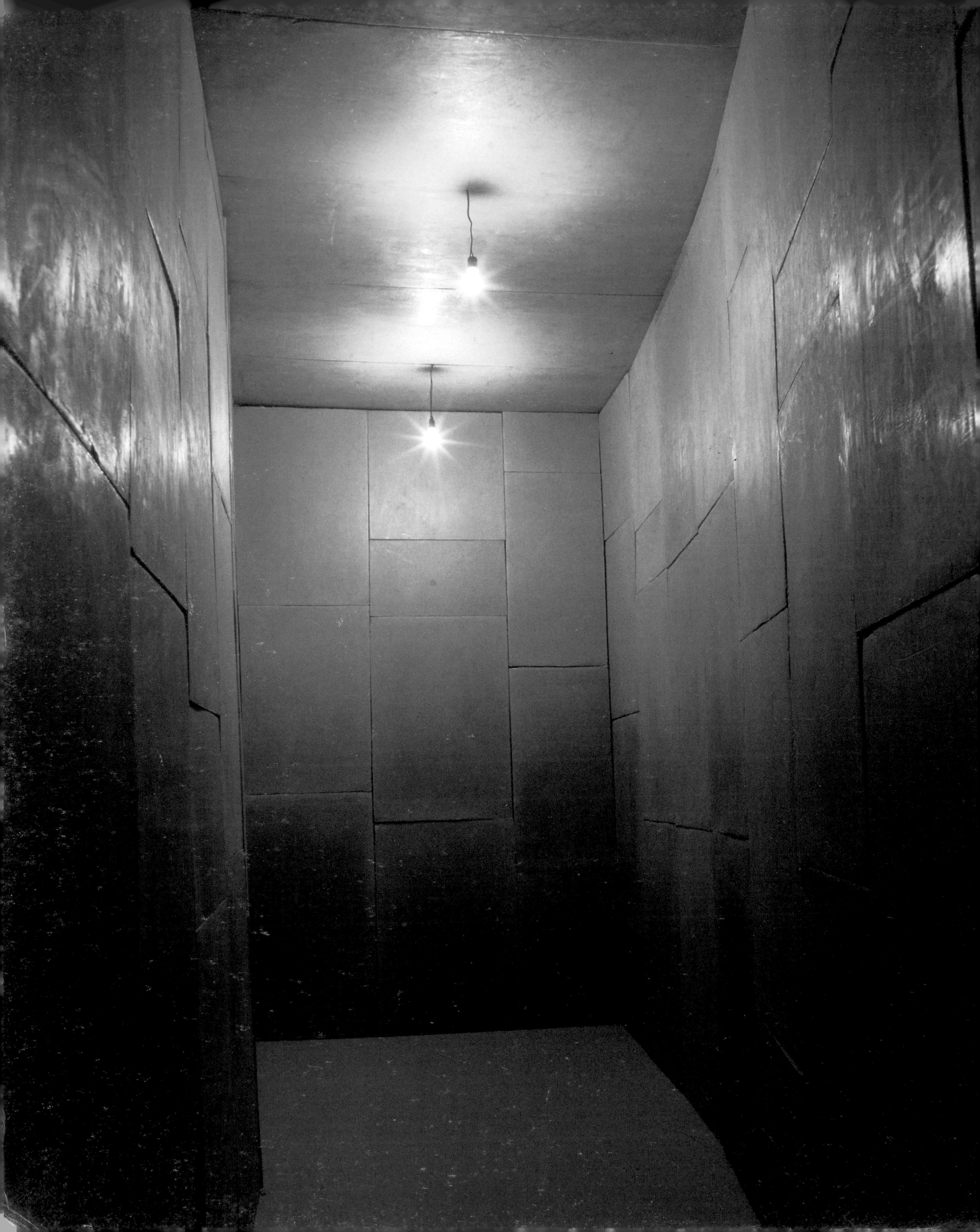

WOLFGANG LAIB

Art has a potential openness, a visionary power which is hardly possible in other areas. I believe that the impossible, the invisible and visions can become reality if one really wants to make the effort. I have probably distanced myself from traditional European ideas of art in every respect.

I think that this is a moment in time in which it is exciting to create something new. It is up to us to do so. There have only been a few moments in time in which that was possible in such an intensive way. It is not just a question of how we treat Nature nor of the condition of Nature, it's do or die, isn't it?

I think that I very quickly detached myself from the concept of time of the European Renaissance culture. Time is not only something linear, but is rather something which recurs – in which a life, an individual no longer begins and ends, in which there is somehow a cycle and a connection with a different time, with a different world and with different bodies. The sole belief in the individual, in one's present body is the energy from which our present culture draws, but it is also its tragedy and its end. Not only in Asian cultures have people thought along much more comprehensive lines. Time is something very different, and somehow, all of that is contained in a milkstone or pollen.

Perhaps there will soon be museums which can deal with very different things and that is certainly urgently needed. And there will also be other places outside of the museums. There are many old works of art which were and are a part of a lived life, which only make sense as part of a ritual – a milkstone is something very similar. For both, a normal museum is just not the right place, but that can be changed.

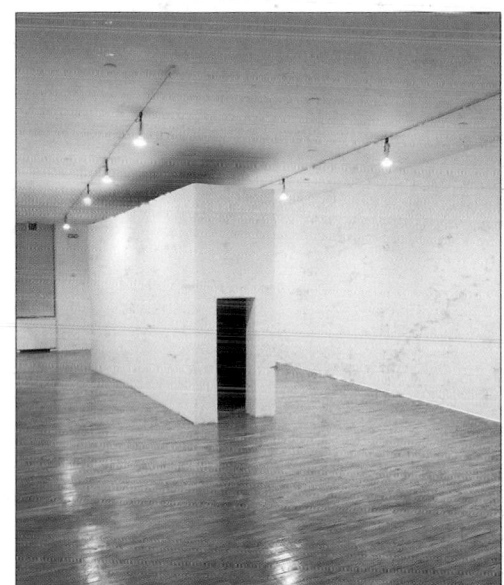

The Passageway, *1988-93, beeswax, wood construction and stucco*

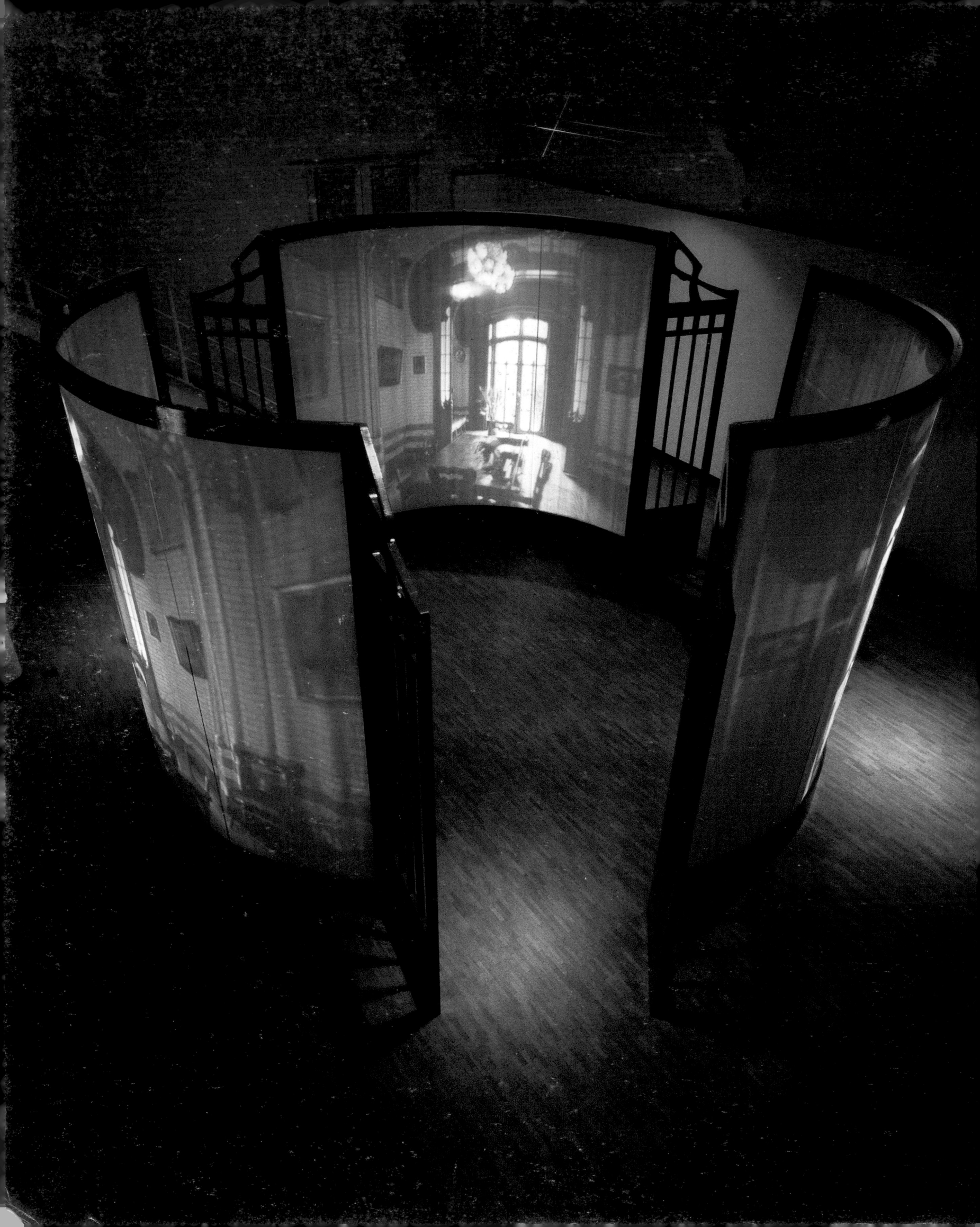

JUDITH BARRY

The Work of the Forest. 'I saw it as though I was dreaming. Perhaps I was. I don't know. I wasn't myself. You and I were waltzing, spinning in the room. When, suddenly, the room became a forest. The chairs turned to trees. The floor, nature's carpet. So green, the smell. For a moment I felt the most complete joy. But then, the trees grew long branches. They encircle my body, not letting me go. I couldn't escape. I thought I would suffocate'. (Charcot patient, quoted in Nelson Abrams, *Charcot's Diary*, London, Samson Press, 1955, p78.)

Walter Benjamin conceived a sense of history that could come to terms with technology and the shifting categories of representations of nature. For him it is the juxtaposition of text and image over time which elucidates historical truth. This 'dialectics of seeing' crystallises antithetical elements by providing axes for their alignment. Using Proust's image of the 'whirling room' as a structuring device, I adapted Benjamin's montage theory to the conflicting histories of Belgian colonial activities in Africa and the particularly Belgian form of Art Nouveau in an endless surround of a continuous pan. It is an appropriate metaphor for examining the ways in which colonial expansion, utopian architecture, *fin-de-siècle* politics and World Fair Ideology intersect, and simultaneously sustain meanings different from and antipathetic to those originally part of their initial histories.

Three large screens, made to fit in a circle with three openings allowing passage to the centre of the circle, comprise the projection area of *The Work of the Forest.* The screen design, based on an Art Nouveau motif, is transparent and can be viewed from several vantage points. Three synchronised videotapes are projected onto the screens showing a continuous panorama. Section 1, set into the ruin of an Art Nouveau house filled with African cultural objects, is a series of ghostly images that come to light as the camera moves. These are historical moments that refer to the history of the relationship between the colonisation of Africa and *fin-de-siècle* life, especially the place of women in domestic space. As the montage elements reappear on the different screens, the viewer hears another sound track, conveying a different history. In this way the spectator can pick and choose among different histories and stories, taking up a variety of subject positions. Each section of the work corresponds to a particular set of issues. Section 2, set in the Stanley Archives, explores the relationships between explorers, traders and missionaries. Section 3, in an Art Nouveau house, concerns the myths of cannibalism and the commodification of African peoples by Europeans. Section 4 contrasts two gardens; the garden King Leopold II of Belgium built for himself to replicate the paradise of Africa, and the garden at the 1897 Congo Exposition where African peoples, living *in situ*, died as they portrayed this (non-) paradise. Section 5 returns to the ruined house, this time running the montage elements in reverse order to show the impossibility of returning to an earlier time, historically. Section 7 continues this idea showing that even with the release of the objects, without a fundamental social transformation that would reorder relations among the classes, history is doomed to repeat itself forever.

The structure of the work is designed to provide several view points or subject positions. From above, the viewer has the comfort and authority most closely associated with monocular perspective and classical Hollywood cinema. From the centre the view is most disorienting, the panorama itself disrupts a sense of closure. From this position it becomes clear that each screen has a different soundtrack, hence the meaning of the images change. A third view from the exterior circumference seems to allow the viewer to predict the sequences seen through the transparent screens, from which one can best deconstruct the competing montage elements.

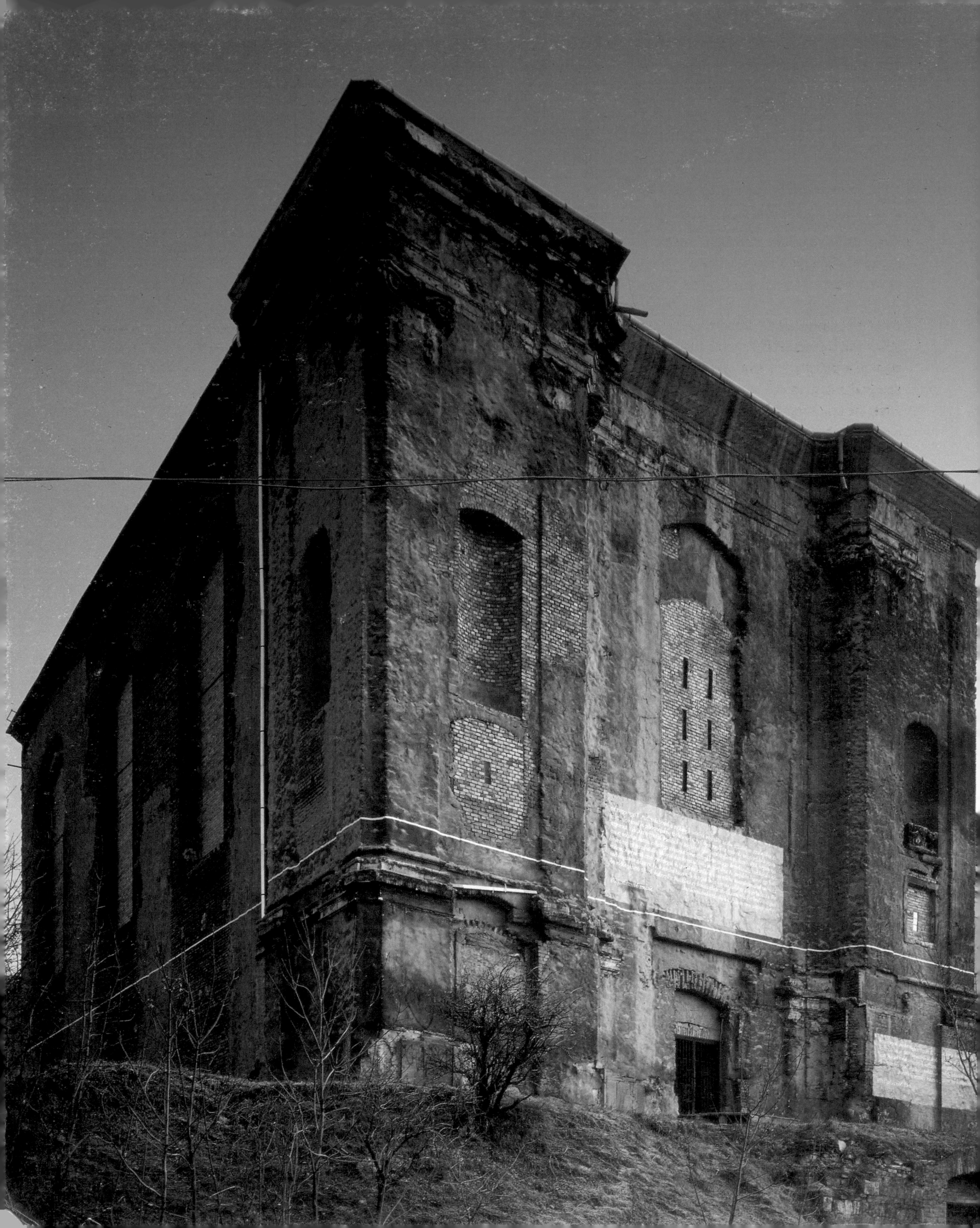

JOSEPH KOSUTH

—Would you restate your understanding of the relationship between art and philosophy, given that you've always defined your work in relation to philosophy?

When art ceased to be defined simply in terms of forms and colours, and began to see itself as a signifying activity, the nature of the practice along with its presumed agenda radically shifted. First, the tendency was to avoid working with elements which were already loaded with meaning as 'art', since this tended to eclipse the signifying project that the artist had in mind. As a result, at least in my case, language itself became both the constructive element and the cultural model simultaneously. The practical implication of this was that context became the organising 'material' around which work formed itself. It became clear that anything could be used, meaningfully, in an art work and that the whole horizon of mass culture within which our consciousness is formed became both a source and a critical location. While philosophy was dying in the academy within a tradition of speculation, art emerged as an activity which could ask questions as it had effect in a world it was part of. Art does not have philosophy's task, this at least partly accounts for its emergence as the most likely candidate to replace it. Philosophy is itself untenable as a philosophical concept.

—How does this relation show itself in your specific art practices, ie in installations?

Installations are fixed. They practise a commitment to a particular location and are largely formed by that context, be it architectural, social, psychological, institutional or whatever. Such work constructs its own 'event context' for the experience of the viewer and in so doing establishes the subjective role of the viewer within the signifying activity as part of the viewer's experience. Beyond the temporary aspect of many, if not most, installations, it is the movability of individual works (which are either actually or a stand-in for painting and sculpture) which now imbued them with a kind of commodity aura. It is the fixed-ness of installations which gives them an actual place in the world and permits that process of signification to function over and above the commodity-reading which so now effects our approach to other kinds of work. In an important way, installations return the language of art to something more akin to 'speech acts' (non-pragmatised, of course) and a change of direction away from gilded illuminations.

ABOVE: American Academy in Rome, *1992; BELOW: Platzverführung, Esslingen, 1992; OPPOSITE: Kisoelli Museum, Budapest, 1993 (photo Láslo Lugosi Lugo); OVERLEAF LEFT AND RIGHT: Passagen-Werk (Documenta Flânerie), June-September 1992, Documenta IX, Kassel*

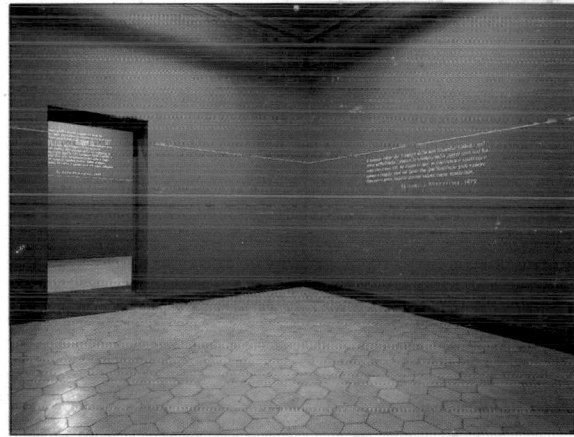

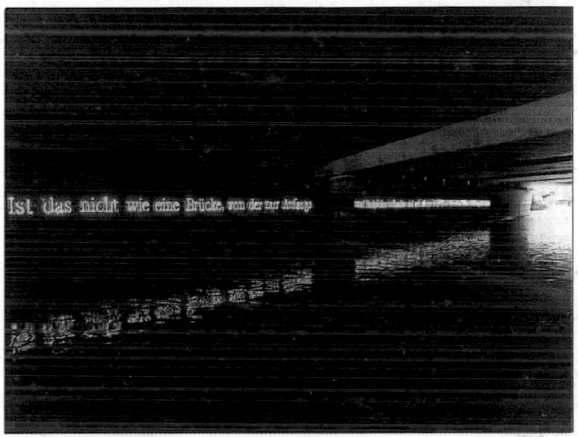

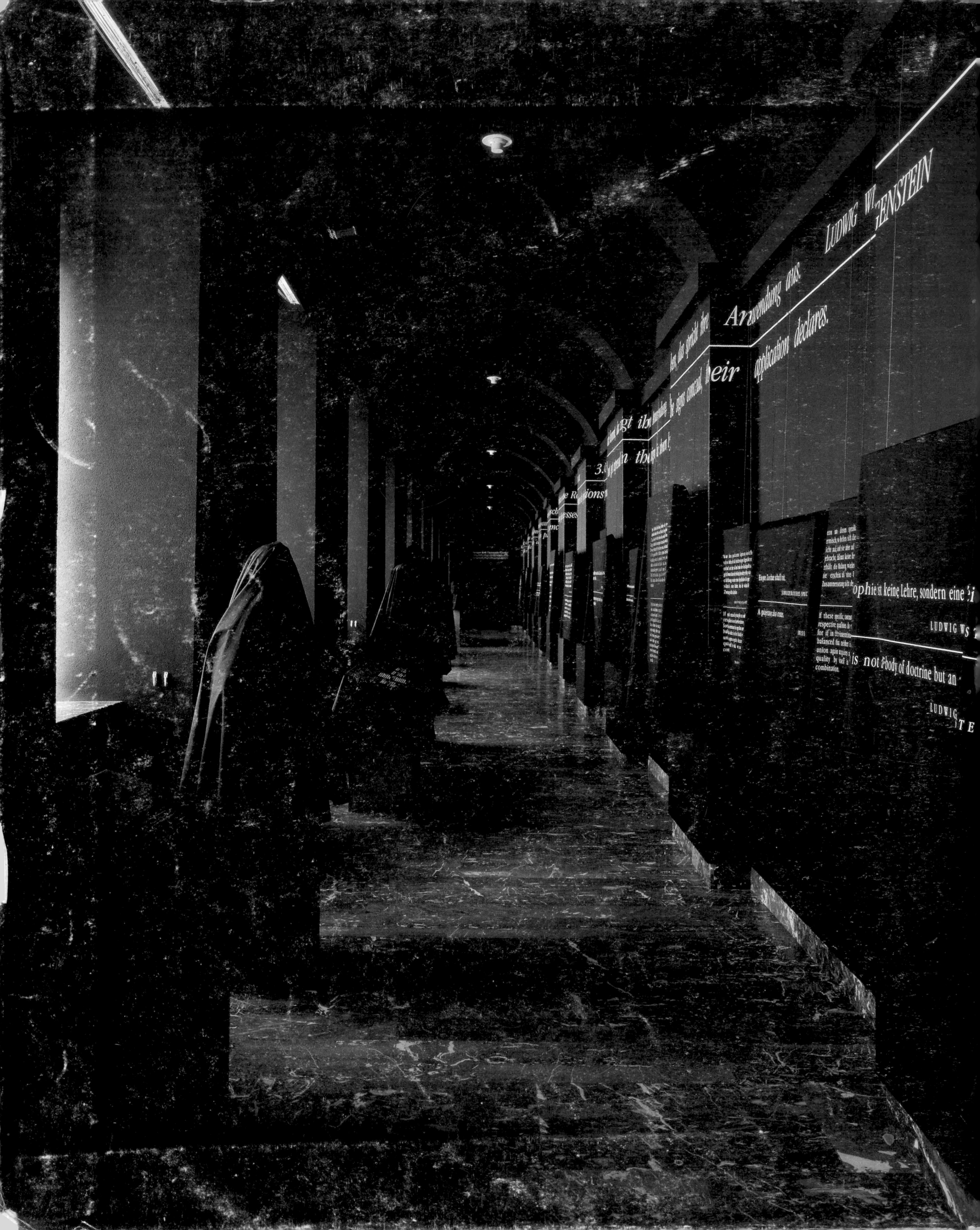